Croydon Transport

MICHAEL H C BAKER

Key Books

TRANSPORT SYSTEMS SERIES, VOLUME 13

Front cover image: Two up-to-date offerings in the much modernised, concreted-over Croydon town centre; in the lead is an Alexander Dennis E40D of Stagecoach Selkent, followed by a Volvo B9TL operated by Metrobus, a Go-Ahead London company. The 403 was for a very long time perhaps the quintessential green bus route, but has been enfolded in recent decades into the red bus network.

Title page image: Centrale tramstop on the Croydon system, 14 March 2024. Nearest the camera is No 2536, one of the original Bombardier CR4000 vehicles of 1998, behind No 2553, a Stadler Variobahn car of 2012.

Back cover image: High Summer 1945, shortly after VE Day, and the residents have brought out their summer attire. Centre stage is Feltham tram No 2090 on its way from the Embankment to Purley with a former Croydon Corporation E1 just visible behind. Behind the Ford Prefect heading in the opposite direction is the celebrated Surrey Street market, whilst opposite, alongside the Feltham, is the Davis Cinema, dating from the late 1920s, and once the largest in the United Kingdom.

Published by Key Books
An imprint of Key Publishing Ltd
PO Box 100
Stamford
Lincs PE9 1XQ

www.keypublishing.com

The right of Michael H C Baker to be identified as the author of this book has been asserted in accordance with the Copyright, Designs and Patents Act 1988 Sections 77 and 78.

Copyright © Michael H C Baker, 2025

ISBN 978 1 80282 861 0

All rights reserved. Reproduction in whole or in part in any form whatsoever or by any means is strictly prohibited without the prior permission of the Publisher.

Typeset by SJmagic DESIGN SERVICES, India.

Introduction

Public transport in Croydon goes back at least to 1086, that is, if the term allows us to include a group of people travelling together on foot or horseback. For, according to the Domesday Book, pilgrims on their way to Canterbury would divert a few miles from up on the North Downs to obtain rest and refreshment in the Croydon settlement of 73 such premises.

Today the media likes to refer to Croydon as a south London suburb, but it was not always so. To be sure, the author's mother did her daily shopping at the Thornton Heath Pond branch of the South Suburban Co-Operative Society; in the understanding of most inhabitants of our area of Thornton Heath Pond, we were living in a suburb of Thornton Heath proper, which in turn was a suburb of Croydon, which was a self-governing county borough set in Surrey. Surrey won the cricket county championship seven times in succession during the 1950s, so we were clearly top dogs. Then there is a long-established Premiership football club, Crystal Palace; capable, if not guaranteed, of beating both Manchester City and Manchester United. When the author was a little lad, Palace's ground, Selhurst Park, was served by Selhurst and Norwood Junction stations, a stone's throw from the Thornton Heath terminus of tram route 42 and served directly by bus route 68, now the 468. Thornton Heath had its own tram depot, which was transformed in 1951 into a bus garage and remains one. Croydon also then and now had its own garage at the South Croydon end of the town, at the Red Deer on the Brighton Road. This had been the old main road from London to Brighton, until Purley Way was opened in 1925, bypassing Croydon to the west. There are two other bus garages in the near locality, both at Beddington. Trams had a depot a little further up the Brighton Road from the Red Deer bus garage, marking the southernmost outpost on the entire London tram network, at that point lying almost in the countryside.

Opened in 1916, Croydon bus garage had originally belonged to Thomas Tilling, hence its designation TC (Tilling Croydon) bestowed by London Transport in 1933. There resided the Tilling-designed petrol-engined ST- and STL-class double-deckers; by 1939, they were due for withdrawal, but the outbreak of war prevented this. On the night of 10/11 May 1941, Croydon suffered the worst damage inflicted on a London bus garage during the war, with seven men killed and 65 buses destroyed. Replacement vehicles, many as old as those destroyed, were brought in from all over the network so that business could be as normal as possible in the morning. As a result, when production of the post-war RT bus began in the late spring of 1947, Croydon, along with Leyton in the northern suburbs, received some of the first, no less than 37 being delivered by the end of the year.

There is no point in trying to gild the lily regarding the problems Croydon is presently facing. The council has just declared effective bankruptcy for the third time in as many years and the Whitgift Centre, the shopping mall built on the site of my old school, Whitgift Middle, in the heart of the town, has been described as 'an empty husk', its floor 'dotted with buckets every time it rains'.

Yet from a transport enthusiast's point of view, there is hardly a more interesting and stimulating place in the land. It has a vast network of bus and tram and train routes that connect the town with just about every part of London, the seaside, the open country and two of the busiest airports in the world.

And if you are still in any doubt, reflect upon the fact that Croydon can claim to have been the home of 'the World's First Public Railway'. Unfortunately, we have to insert the phrase 'Contrary to General Belief', ahead of this. It all depends what you mean both by 'public' and 'railway'. We were certainly decades ahead of both the Stockton and Darlington and the Liverpool and Manchester railways. Both these used steam power, the

Croydon Transport

Stockton and Darlington still placing some reliance on the horse. Rails of some description may even have been used by the Greeks and Romans, if we are prepared to accept the definition that 'a railway or trackway is a device that does not let the carriage come off the track.' Up above Goathland on the North Yorkshire Moors, it is possible to walk along a Roman trackway that may have been deliberately created, where carts followed grooves worn in the stones.

The valley of the Wandle, the river that flows through the centre of Croydon, is largely unseen today, but had been described at the beginning of the 19th century as 'the most heavily industrialised area in the south of England'. The Wandle rises in South Croydon, close to the foothills of the North Downs – let us not stray into Himalayan metaphors; we're dealing with inches, or centimetres if you prefer. When I was a trainee reporter on the *Croydon Advertiser* in 1955, I attended an enquiry into environmental matters, which were beginning to be of concern (although few had opposed the replacement of the electric tram by the bus running on imported diesel, nor would they object too vociferously at the end of the decade to the removal of Croydon's trolleybuses) and an elderly gentleman described how in his youth, salmon were found in the Wandle. That seemed inconceivable in the mid-1950s; the muddy trench that the river was by then was a hair's-breadth from a sewer. A decade later, my father worked for a time as a Wandle Park keeper, a task he did not much enjoy. There had been a lake and a bandstand there, but the water supply was very iffy and it all became very run down and neglected. However, in 2012, the local authority belatedly stepped up, putting a great deal of time, money and effort into turning Wandle Park into something of which the borough could be proud.

The 8¼-mile-long Surrey Iron Railway was established by an Act of Parliament in 1801, linking Croydon with Wandsworth. It wasn't a railway as we understand the term today; the rails were L-shaped so that the wheels, which were ordinary wagon wheels, ran between the iron rails, which were fixed to stone blocks. The gauge was 4ft 2in. Cast-iron plateway might more accurately describe it. The railway company owned the track, but carriers supplied their own wagons and horses and paid tolls. Wagons had to be of a stipulated design and size, rather like a modern container; they registered with the railway company and had to have their number and name painted in 3ft-high white numerals on a black background. Speed depended on the pace of the horse, as on a canal. It was possible for a horse, or a mule, to pull several wagons, exemplifying one of the advantages of a fixed, relatively smooth track.

All sorts of industries along the Wandle Valley made use of the railway; coal, as one would expect, plus corn, seeds, manure, lime and building materials. Before the railway, there had been plans for a canal, but as we have seen, the water supply in the Wandle Valley could not be relied on. The eventual railway sprouted various short branches and, as on the 'proper' railways, a number of level crossings. Pavement stones ensured that the level was maintained and there were even points worked by a pivoted iron rail, which enabled wagons to change tracks and enter sidings.

The Wandsworth end of the railway boasted a series of complex facilities. A wharf connected to the Thames could accommodate 30 barges, into which the railway wagons could transfer their load, and locks permitted the transit of large vessels, such as Medway sailing barges. These were so common on the Thames that they were still plying their trade, mostly downriver from the Pool of London, when the Southend-bound paddle steamers resumed their excursions from Tower Pier after World War Two. Our family took great enjoyment in these trips.

Another part of the story of the immediate pre-steam railway period is that of the Croydon Canal, which opened in 1809. This began at what is now West Croydon station, and ran through South Norwood, Sydenham and on by way of 28 locks to Rotherhithe and thence to the Thames. Beside it was a railway (plateway) that connected with the Croydon, Merstham and Godstone Railway. This had opened in 1805, its design based on the Surrey Iron Railway, and was constructed chiefly to serve quarries in the Merstham area. For a while, this made a profit, as did the canal and the Surrey Iron Railway, although they were in competition and this would eventually bring about the demise of all of them, a process completed by the conversion of the Croydon Canal to a railway in 1839. None of these concerns, as far as is known, ever carried passengers.

Croydon Transport

George Stephenson now enters the story, or, to be precise, was invited by a director of the Surrey Iron Railway to construct a locomotive. However, on checking the feasibility of the cast-iron plateway, he realised that it simply could not support the weight of a steam locomotive and declined. Presumably, conversion to a Liverpool and Manchester-style proper railway was never a possibility.

The first steam railway to obtain an Act of Parliament to reach Croydon was the London and Croydon in 1836. In December of that year, the London and Greenwich, the first railway south of the Thames, opened its terminus at London Bridge. At that time, it was thought that London Bridge would be adequate for all railways south of the Thames, just as it was considered that Euston would be the only one needed north of the river. Few saw just how universal railways would become and how rapidly, but one party that did plan ahead, the London and Croydon, arranged to buy some of the land at the not-yet-opened London Bridge terminus. In yet another 1836 development, the South Eastern Railway received authorisation to build a line from Croydon to Dover, using the London and Croydon's tracks out of London Bridge. The following year, the London and Brighton Railway obtained its Act, allowing it also to run over the Croydon Railway's tracks from Norwood. So rapid was this all taking place that the London and Greenwich was given parliamentary powers for what was almost certainly the first four-track railway in the country, and probably the world, on the elevated approach to London Bridge.

The London and Croydon Railway bought the Croydon Canal for £40,250, intending to drain it and use its bed as the trackbed. However, this turned out to be much more complicated and expensive than originally envisaged, as the canal was very winding, and a number of gradients had to be contended with, notably around New Cross and also skirting the Sydenham Heights. Here was where the Crystal Palace would be transported from Hyde Park and re-erected after the Great Exhibition of 1851 came to an end. This awe-inspiring structure much influenced the railway network and its fame led to the area adopting its name as its own.

The cost that the London and Greenwich Railway imposed on its tenants was perceived as excessive by them and brought about a search for an alternative terminus for both passenger and goods traffic. Bricklayers Arms, a mile or so to the south of London Bridge, was chosen, opening in 1844, and was also briefly used for passenger traffic by the South Eastern Railway. That proved to be a mistake, as Bricklayers Arms was a working-class, unfashionable area of London and distant from where most passengers to the capital wished to find themselves. It closed in 1852, but remained ideal for goods traffic, flourishing in that role; indeed, a large locomotive depot was opened and was used by passenger and freight locomotives working in and out of London Bridge, Cannon Street and Charing Cross for as long as steam survived. The locomotives off Oxted-line trains, for instance, were the only steam examples regularly serving East Croydon in British Railways days, and were serviced at Bricklayers Arms (73B). Goods traffic finally came to an end there in 1981.

Although steam was in the ascendancy by the 1840s, other forms of motive power were mooted, and one that attracted much attention by seeming to promise vastly less pollution, quietness of operation, and no need for any form of locomotive, was the atmospheric railway. A piston beneath the train fitted into a pipe laid between the rails of the running track and the air was drawn out so that the pressure propelled the train. The best-known proponent of the system was Isambard Kingdom Brunel, who used it in South Devon. It was also applied between Kingstown and Dalkey in Ireland. Least well remembered, however, was Croydon's experiment, which was tried out between West Croydon and South Norwood in 1846. For a brief while, the system worked and promised much, but the technology to ensure that the vacuum could be maintained 100 per cent of the time simply did not exist. The experiment lasted little more than a year and is said to have cost the Croydon Railway £500,000. By that time, this railway had amalgamated with others to form the London, Brighton and South Coast Railway, which would survive until absorbed into the Southern Railway in the 1923 Grouping.

Croydon Transport

Meanwhile, the Surrey Iron Railway closed on 31 August 1846. Although the valley between Croydon and Wandsworth along which it had run was, indeed, accurately described as the 'Most Heavily Industrialised Area in Southern England', it was a small-scale, pre-Industrial Revolution world, dependent upon the efforts of man, of horses and wind and water power. Time had moved on and it was no longer profitable. There were no coal mines in Croydon; it was not the sort of heavily industrialised area that could compete with the vast industries of South Wales, the Midlands, the North-East, the North-West or the Clyde Estuary.

This is not to say that nothing of it remains, or that it is forgotten. If you prepare to board a tram at Reeves Corner at the bottom of Church Street, Croydon, you will be standing on the site of the Surrey Iron Railway's terminus. Once aboard, you will pass around the edge of Wandle Park, plunge into the heart of what was once Croydon Gas Works, and dive under the A23 Brighton Road, noting the twin towers marking IKEA, all that is left of Power Station B where a saddle tank still shunted coal wagons in 1970. Crossing Beddington Lane, which really was a rural lane as late as the 1960s on the edge of Mitcham Common, and where a donkey might look up to note the passing two-coach train, you then join the point at Mitcham Junction where through trains to the Sussex Coast passed on the opposite platform. Today, Tramway Path marks where the Iron Railway's Hackbridge branch ran. Onward past a pig farm to Mitcham which, it is claimed, is 'the oldest continuously working station site in the world', you penetrate back into the deep greenery of the grounds of Morden Park, watered by the Wandle and now owned by the National Trust. Here a snuff mill operated until around the time the Underground, in the shape of the Northern Line, arrived in 1926 at the end of what was then the longest railway tunnel in the world. Our tram journey ends at Tramlink's own platform in Wimbledon station, but the Surrey Iron Railway continued on to Wandsworth. We might care to board a Waterloo-bound stopping train, change at Clapham Junction and take a short ride back to where the Wandle passes under the railway and enters the Thames.

Before Tramlink, there was the 5¾-mile-long West Croydon to Wimbledon line, opened on 22 October 1855, just nine years after the Surrey Iron Railway closed. It was leased to the London, Brighton and South Coast Railway (LB&SCR) a year later and absorbed by that undertaking in 1866. For most of its short route, it followed that of the Surrey Iron Railway. It was single-track and initially saw only six passenger trains a day, though freight played a significant part. Push-pull working took over in 1919, and, despite its existence being under threat at times, the line was electrified in July 1930. This ensured its survival, although other third-rail SR lines ultimately closed, notably those to Crystal Palace High Level and Haywards Heath to Horsted Keynes. The carriages of the Southern Railway's suburban multiple-units were nearly all converted steam stock, and those provided for the West Croydon to Wimbledon line were no exception. Numbered 1809–1812, they were formed from original LB&SCR overhead electric first class carriages and, although downgraded, something of their original upmarket ambience remained, as well as side gangways, so they were quite different to the usual run of EMUs. The steam locomotives that worked goods traffic on the line were also of LB&SCR design, comprising C2X 0-6-0s and various 0-6-2Ts. One of the latter, an E4 originally named *Birch Grove*, has been preserved by the Bluebell Railway. The coal trains serving the gas works and power station B were usually hauled by the big, powerful W-class 2-6-4Ts, being replaced when diesels took over by the Class 33 Cromptons, which remained until coal firing ended in 1984.

The official boundary between London proper and Croydon, the River Graveney, was just north of Norbury railway station, down the hill from Streatham. The Graveney flowed into the Wandle, which in turn flowed into the Thames at Wandsworth. The Graveney extended for no more than 5½ miles, so it was nothing to get excited about, but it was 'our' Graveney, in that one of its few exposed stretched, not too much grander than a drain, in fact, flowed along the edge of the 'Rec', the recreation ground at the end of Winterbourne Road Primary School, which your author attended from 1946 to 1948.

Apart from tram depots and bus garages, Croydon boasted a large electric train depot at Selhurst, which is still there, plus a steam locomotive depot just beyond Norwood Junction; this also acquired diesels early on. Electrification, beginning before World War One, had meant the elimination of a number of small locomotive depots in the area, although the actual building of at least one, at Purley, survives.

Croydon Transport

Croydon was served by trams, trains and motor buses, but also by trolleybuses. In the most recent decade, electrically powered buses have once again plied the streets of Croydon, although no overhead street wires are involved these days, so they can't be called trolleybuses. In the heyday of such operations prior to 1961, there were the 654s, which ran between Crystal Palace and Sutton, and the 630s, which ran between West Croydon and that most extraordinary destination on the entire London Transport network, 'Near Willesden Junction'. The 654s lived at a depot at Carshalton, to the west of Croydon, the 630s far away at Shepherd's Bush. Both these routes had replaced tram equivalents in the 1930s. There had also once been a tram depot at Aurelia Road, Thornton Heath. This ceased operations when the 30 tram route ended in 1936 and later served as a site for the breaking up of trams. A macabre use during World War Two was as a morgue for those killed in the Blitz, in which Croydon suffered grievously. The depot for the modern Tramlink is no great distance away, just a few hundred metres across the Mitcham Road, along which the 30 trams and the 630 trolleybuses once plied their trade.

We have not yet exhausted all that Croydon had to offer the transport buff. Once the war was over, Green Line coaches reappeared and soon, by the end of June 1946, five routes were running along the main road past the Pond, through the centre of Croydon and then fanning out southwards into the Surrey, Kent and Sussex countrysides to terminate at Crawley, East Grinstead, Godstone, Westerham and Oxted. In the opposite direction, their journeys took them through the heart of the West End to the Chilterns and some excellent fox-hunting territory, if you were into that sort of thing, at Amersham, Chesham, Aylesbury, and Hemel Hempstead. In July 1953, an orbital route, the 725, was introduced between Windsor and Gravesend, by way of Croydon. A substantial proportion sidestepped the later running down of Green Line and survived into the modern era as route 726 and then X26, before being relaunched spectacularly in 2023 as Superloop SL7, connecting Croydon with Heathrow to the west. One could argue that Green Line vehicles were glorified buses rather than true coaches, designed to London Transport's very specific requirements, but, at the other end of the scale, there was no doubting that the pinnacle of luxury belonged to the splendid Harrington-bodied Leyland Tiger coaches of Southdown, which passed Thornton HeathPond each day, and would stop at the newsagent there if booked beforehand, on their way from Victoria coach station to the Sussex coast.

Croydon's position on the direct route between London and fashionable Brighton, not too far distant, meant that by the beginning of the 19th century, it was probably attracting more regular stagecoach traffic than any other road in England; 52 such vehicles each day in 1815. All had ceased by 1845, however, wiped out by the London, Brighton and South Coast Railway, and it wasn't until the end of World War One and the associated great advances in motor vehicle technology and improvements in road layout and surfacing, that the railways were faced with a serious rival in the form of the charabanc, or motor coach. The first Southdown coaches began on the Brighton route in 1920. At weekends, they were joined by a flotilla of coaches belonging to such well-known fleets as Orange Coaches of Brixton, Grey Green of Catford and Valliant of Ealing. Then there were Croydon's own Bourne & Balmer and John Bennett coach companies.

To the immediate south was the Country Area of London Transport. To quote Peter Aves in his definitive *Green All Over*, 'The most intense [Country Area] services of all were the trunk routes radiating out from Croydon across the whole of the southern area.' In 1955, 93 green buses from nine garages, the equivalent of many a provincial company's entire fleet, were scheduled to ply the streets of Croydon on Monday to Friday, with slight variations at weekends. By that date, they were all RTs, the once almost as numerous STLs and their own ST predecessors having all been withdrawn. A green bus would take you as far into Kent as Westerham, Sevenoaks and Tonbridge, and into Sussex to East Grinstead, Forest Row, Crawley and Horsham.

Finally, we arrive at Croydon Aerodrome, which lasted a mere 44 years but in its heyday made Croydon world famous. Starting in 1915 as a grass strip beside Purley Way, then a country lane before its later promotion to become the main A23 London to Brighton Road, this facility was designated the London Terminal Aerodrome in March 1920. As planes are wont to do, it took off instantly. Given the limited range of early aircraft, most commercial services were to Paris, Brussels and elsewhere on the continent. The railways played their part in helping pilots, often seated in open cockpits, find their way by painting the names of the stations at Redhill, Tonbridge and Ashford on their roofs as the aircraft followed the railway lines to the coast, and this practice was also followed on the other side of the Channel. Despite being expensive, not very comfortable and often hazardous, flying was the thing to do, and just about anyone who was anyone would come down to Croydon, usually in a hire car, and take to the air. It was suggested that Waddon station, just down the road on the West Croydon to Sutton branch, should rename itself 'Waddon for London Airport,' but this never happened. The future King George VI learned to fly from Croydon, and Winston Churchill, Charlie Chaplin, Charles Lindbergh, Amy Johnson and countless other celebrities were all seen there. The greatest crowd ever at an airport, until the Beatles at Heathrow in 1963, greeted Lindbergh at Croydon after his first solo flight across the Atlantic, on 29 May 1927. Later that evening, the town experienced its biggest traffic jam so far with 2,000 motorists and motorcyclists struggling to get home. By 1938, planes were flying from Croydon to destinations all over the world, including swastika-marked Junkers Ju 52 airliners direct to and from Berlin.

Immediately on the outbreak of war, all commercial flying in and out of Croydon ceased and the RAF took over. Spitfires and Hurricanes became the norm, while the swastika again became a familiar sight as the Battle of Britain was fought above Croydon's skies. Though aviation made enormous strides during the war, housing had sprung up all around the airport, preventing expansion, and the four-engined airliners coming into service post-war needed longer runways. What had once been the world's first and greatest airport thus went into decline. DC-3s, Dragon Rapides, Doves and Herons operated commercial services for a while, but soon moved on to Heathrow, Northolt or Gatwick. Croydon Airport closed in 1959. Its handsome Grade II-listed terminal, now an office building, remains as a reminder of the glory days, as does the control tower.

Trams ceased serving Croydon in 1951, but a new system, Tramlink, began in the year 2000 and remains the only tram system in the London area so far. Trolleybuses in turn disappeared in 1961. The return of the tram marked the fruition of years of careful, well-argued persuasion by a few dedicated people, both professional and amateur. Not the least of their arguments was that the extensive development of council houses up on the windy heights above Addington, which began just before World War Two, needed better links with central Croydon. As with so many schemes to move people out of what were considered substandard town and city centre dwellings to something better far away on the outskirts throughout the land, the people affected were not consulted. Even so, a fast, frequent limited-stop service on rails into the heart of Croydon and beyond definitely had its attractions, and adapting under-used rail lines would also be an integral part of the scheme, in theory bringing down costs.

Thus came Tramlink, operated by slinky, German-built, articulated 70-seat trams. Its New Addington route emerges from the estate on reserved tracks laid parallel to the hill from New Addington, crossing the Selsdon to West Wickham Road by Addington village. Then, heading parallel to the road up to Shirley Hills and down again alongside Coombe Road, the line takes over the trackbed of the Selsdon to Elmers End railway line, proceeding through its tunnel at Sandilands. From there, the trams shares road space with other traffic along Addiscombe Road to East Croydon, heading onward into George Street, past the Tudor alms houses in the heart of the town, and down Crown Hill, which had never seen public transport before. On through Old Town, past Reeves Corner, which had once been the terminus of the Surrey Iron Railway, the trams then arrive at Wandle Park a little further on. Here they assume the trackbed of the West Croydon to Wimbledon line, deviating from this route's historical path only for the last few hundred yards before gaining their own platform at Wimbledon station. Evidently, there was nowhere suitable in Wimbledon for an on-street tram terminus, although there had been once upon a time, when routes 2 and 4 connected it with the Victoria Embankment.

Eastward from Wandle Park, the trams head past Reeves Corner, up along Tamworth Road and then thread their way alongside West Croydon rail and bus stations. Passing the back of the Whitgift Centre, they rejoin the westbound route by the Park Lane/George Street underpass. Tramlink also took over railway lines from

Sandilands to Beckenham Junction and Elmers End, getting tantalisingly close to Crystal Palace, but never reaching it. Despite numerous studies to this end and millions spent in the process, Tramlink ever has never been extended to Sutton, another obvious local destination with more space to accommodate trams than there appears.

The Country Area of London Transport became London Country, part of the National Bus Company (NBC) in 1970, but further railway electrification and increasing car use has led to the virtual elimination of the network as we knew it then. The Warlingham Road, once served by five routes, now has just one, the 403, which is still very busy, and, logically, is now worked by red buses. Beyond Chelsham, there are no regular bus services any more. Traffic congestion has meant that the only bus routes that now link Croydon with central London are the night-time N68 and the rush-hour Superloop SL6, formerly known as X68. We can also, just about, include the 3. Since 2023, this route's central London terminus has been Victoria, while its long-established southern endpoint at Crystal Palace lies within yards of where Croydon meets historic Kent. Incidentally, at one time it seemed likely that Tramlink would find itself extended up Anerley Hill to Crystal Palace, logically joining the focal point of several routes terminating here. It may yet happen.

Though the railway situation has changed less dramatically in the post-World War Two years than that of road transport, it has kept pace with the changing world around it. West Croydon and East Croydon remain the two principal stations connecting the town with the West End and the City of London, as well as various points south, east and west. In 1945, and for some years afterwards, the West End and the City were the furthest north the train would take you, but now you can travel directly over or under the Thames every few minutes, on to St Pancras. From there comes a great range of connections in all directions, encompassing the old Midland main line to Bedford, the Great Northern to Peterborough, the Great Eastern to Cambridge or, by way of Shepherds Bush, to Watford Junction and Hemel Hempstead. Of course, the question then arises as to who would have wanted to travel without changing from Croydon to Hemel Hempstead or Bedford? As we have seen, Hemel Hempstead was also the terminus of Green Line 708, though this was more for operational than passenger convenience.

There were plenty of steam locomotives to be seen in the Croydon area in 1945, although they were far outnumbered by electric multiple-units. The former mostly worked freight; coal trains to the power station at Waddon, for instance, generated so much business that a separate line was provided from West Croydon, around the edge of Wandle Park, to keep them clear of the passenger services. The coal trains were the preserve of the W Class 2-6-4Ts. The passenger service, meanwhile, was worked by the Two Trains, so-called threefold because only two units were needed to maintain the service, the headcode on the former London, Brighton and South Coast veterans that worked them was 2, and each unit consisted of two carriages.

Plenty of of goods yards were still attached to the various stations dotted around the borough, mostly for the coal business, although whether they were making a profit is debatable. They provided employment for elderly former LB&SCR 0-6-2Ts, but there was nothing remarkable about this, as ex-Brighton locomotives proliferated on both goods and passenger trains, far outnumbering those of Southern Railway origin. Main line goods featured the C2X 0-6-0s and the L B Billington-designed K Class 2-6-0s. These latter also worked passenger trains, as did the D3 0-4-4Ts, while the Oxted line, which was worked exclusively by steam, was home to former main line express locomotives displaced by electrification. There were the last of the B4 4-4-0s, nice-looking but fairly feeble, and the handsome B4X rebuilds, themselves not very much better. The most famous ex-Brighton locomotives, the diminutive Stroudley Terrier 0-6-0Ts, were not much seen in the Croydon area. The Marsh-designed I3 4-4-2Ts, which had established such a reputation for themselves in their Edwardian heyday, were being withdrawn, but still appeared on Oxted line passenger duties, as did the two handsome Billington 4-6-2Ts. Once, long ago, the South Eastern Railway had shared with the London, Brighton and South Coast Railway the main line from London Bridge as far as Redhill, and one or two survivors from those days remained in the form of an early morning train calling at East Croydon, Redhill and then turning left to

Tonbridge and on to the Kent Coast. There were also one or two steam-hauled trains that divided at Redhill, with one section heading into Kent and the other to Reading via Guildford.

Former SE&SCR locomotives were to be seen at East Croydon, particularly on Oxted line trains. A succession of inside-cylinder 4-4-0s, ranging from the Wainwright D, E and L classes to the final, long-lived D1 and E1 rebuilds also put in appearances on the Redhill to Brighton main line. Lasting almost until the end of steam were the H Class 0-4-4Ts and the C Class 0-6-0s. A surprising veteran was former South Eastern Railway Stirling-designed O1 class 0-6-0 No 31048 of 1878, which appeared as late as May 1959 on station pilot duties at East Croydon.

Then there were the Brighton Atlantics, fabulous engines of H1 and H2 classes, which worked both the Oxted line and often, through Brighton services, plus the celebrated Newhaven boat trains, carrying the legend 'Continental Express'. Sometimes, they came complete with Pullmans, which elevated them into the very top rank. The H2s were destined to be the last operational Atlantics on British Railways, and although none was preserved, a replica *Beachy Head* has been completed in the Bluebell Railway workshops.

With its emphasis on electrification, the Southern Railway built relatively few steam locomotives. The N and U1 2-6-0s, derived from SE&CR Maunsell designs, were perhaps the most often encountered in the Croydon area on both passenger and goods duties. The occasional L1 4-4-0 put in an appearance, while top of the range was the powerful Schools Class 4-4-0. Former LB&SCR-built locomotives continued on the 'Southern Belle' until electrification in 1933 and its renaming as the 'Brighton Belle', which passed through East Croydon but didn't normally stop there. Bulleid Q1 Class 0-6-0s were joined right at the end of the steam era, by Bulleid Light Pacifics. The Southern built three main-line electric locomotives, which were seen regularly in the Croydon area working both the Newhaven boat train and heavy freights.

Finally, there were the British Railways standard designs. The handsome 4MT 2-6-4Ts were built at Brighton and almost established a monopoly on the Oxted line until the end of steam, replacing the LMS-designed Brighton-built locomotives of the same wheel arrangement. Limited use was also made of the Class 2MT 2-6-2Ts and the Standard 4MT 4-6-0s.

OPPOSITE ABOVE: This is the actual frontier between London and Croydon, or it certainly was when this photograph was taken around 1910. The child, sucking its thumb – some things never change – beside its state-of-the-art perambulator and mother, is actually standing on the bridge over the River Graveney that marked the border, so that the photographer, probably equipped with a tripod because the hand-held Kodak Brownie had only just been invented, is in Norbury, as is E1-type tram No 1067 of the London County Council (LCC). E1s first took to the tracks in 1907, continued in production until 1930 and remained at work until 1952. A very sound investment, but it also meant that vehicles dating back to Edwardian times were in competition with the RT motor bus, also still in production in 1952. On either side of the road in this picture are signs advertising Croydon Corporation trams, one of which can be seen in the distance about to pass under the railway bridge at Norbury. With its four wheels and open top, it was already dated. Until February 1926, through passengers had to dismount from an LCC tram and cross the bridge to climb aboard the Croydon one.

OPPOSITE BELOW: Arriva London South Leyland Olympian L 255 passing beneath Norbury railway bridge in November 2001, the same bridge seen in the far distance in the previous picture. Behind is another Olympian on route 109, which in 1951 replaced tram routes 16/18 connecting the Embankment with Purley, but has been cut down in length over the years.

DRAPERS
SOMERSET HOUSE VIA WESTMINSTER
1027

FOOD & WINE
OPEN TILL LATE
FOOD & WINE
WINES-BEERS-SPIRITS-GROCERIES
OFF LICENCE
50
SOUTH CROYDON
ARRIVA
D255 FYM

4-SUB No 4705 passes over this bridge as it slows to enter Norbury station with a Victoria to Coulsdon North stopping train in 1968.

The same location in 2015. The Class 377s, known as Electrostars, made their debut in 2001, the inaugural examples being built at Derby. Composed of open carriages with through connections and limited First Class accommodation, although the seats were no more luxurious than those in the rest of the train, they were intended for long distance work. They remained in production until 2014 and in practice are also regularly employed on suburban duties, as here.

A line of trams, consisting of Felthams and various varieties of E1, caught en route between Croydon and Telford Avenue in the aftermath of one of the dreadful winter of 1947's snowstorms.

A Dennis Dart of Arriva London South at Pollards Hill in November 2001, about to continue on its way to the 255's Clapham Common terminus of that time. Manufactured from 1989, the Dart single-decker was a phenomenally successful product, the Guildford-based manufacturer building more than 12,000 in both step-entrance and SLF form in an 18-year period. The route, based at Thornton Heath garage, was introduced on 29 August 1998. It has varied somewhat over the years and from the beginning of 2025 has started tentatively converting to electric buses. Note the advert for the Whitgift Centre, a huge shopping mall built in the heart of Croydon on the site of Whitgift Middle School, which moved out to Shirley Park in 1968.

Green Lane runs from Norbury to Thornton Heath High Street, roughly parallel to the main A23 London Road, and until around 1930 a sliver of countryside there separated the County Borough of Croydon from London. Green Lane lives up to its name here as a number 50 heads for Thornton Heath in 2005.

The very last working Atlantic was No 32424 *Beachy Head*. It had spent its long career on the Brighton line, and here it is performing for the final time on 13 April 1958 on a special train of boat train stock, speeding through Norbury towards Newhaven. Despite efforts to preserve *Beachy Head*, it was broken up after this run. However, many years later the boiler of a virtually identical GNR large Atlantic was discovered and was brought to Sheffield Park on the Bluebell Railway, where a workshop was provided for the construction of a replica. In the summer of 2024, this took to the rails.

The same location some 50 years later, as No 66717 heads northwards with a train of ballast for the London Underground. The Class 66s are the workhorses of modern UK freight. Built by the Electro-Motive Diesel division of General Motors, more than 500 were delivered from 1996 onwards, some serving in mainland Europe.

One of the big vintage transport events of the year is the Historic Commercial Vehicle Club's road run each spring from London to Brighton. This usually starts from Crystal Palace and heads down to Streatham Common, where it joins the A23. During the May 1995 event, a former Southdown Titan double-deck bus converted to a recovery vehicle is leading the one and only surviving six-wheel London Transport AEC Renown double-decker, LT 165, past Thornton Heath Pond. Together they are overtaking a parked 1930s vintage Leyland fire engine. Southdown coaches were a regular sight here, connecting the Sussex coast with Victoria Coach Station: their National Express Coach successors still are. LTs were not normally seen in the vicinity of Thornton Heath, however; the only route to be seen on this section of the A23 for many years was the 115, which was worked by buses from Croydon and Sutton, using D-class austerity Daimlers, STs and briefly, post-war all-Leyland PD1s (STD class) before the all-conquering RT took over. The 115 itself lasted until 1981.

Tram No 1 as preserved in London Transport livery working route 16. This was the only truly modern tram ever introduced by the London County Council, shortly before the absorption of that body's bus operations into those of the London Passenger Transport Board in 1933. London Transport was committed to abolishing the tram and, like an unwanted orphan, No 1 lived a lonely life amongst the equally modern Felthams at Telford Avenue or the adjoining Brixton Hill depot, appearing only at rush hour and on special occasions. It was sold to Leeds with the Felthams, eventually entering preservation at the National Tram Museum at Crich, where its restoration to original LCC condition has just been completed.

Former Croydon Corporation E1 No 388 is about to turn out of Brigstock Road into London Road, c1949. The wooded slopes of Upper Norwood mark the horizon. The 42 was one of only two tram routes (the other was the 44) that, post-1945, did not serve central London. It took just 20 minutes to connect Thornton Heath High Street with Coombe Road, Croydon, cars running every three to four minutes during normal weekdays. Schoolboys knew that there were certain locations where those sitting in the sideways-facing seats upstairs could experience a most amusing series of bounces.

A Feltham departs Thornton Heath Pond c1950, neck-and-neck with a Standard Flying Eight, on a rush-hour working back to Telford Avenue depot. The Feltham was the Pullman of the tram fleet, many considering their ride quality the equal of the RT.

A 4-SUB arriving at Thornton Heath station in 1970. The high-capacity, steel-bodied Bulleid-designed 4-SUB EMUs were introduced in 1941 and went into full-scale production immediately after the war. Not particularly comfortable, their great quality was their capacity, a boon to the operating authorities and commuters alike. They were the backbone of the Southern's suburban network for decades, the last ones being taken out of service in 1983.

ABOVE: Seen from the down slow platform at Thornton Heath in 1970, the rather handsome and substantial station dates from the early 1900s, when the tracks between Selhurst and Balham were quadrupled. The fast line platforms are no longer used and much of the building, although intact, is redundant.

RIGHT: Thornton Heath's down slow platform in 2018. There were originally goods yards on both sides of the station, but once coal traffic ceased in the 1960s, they were taken out of use.

ABOVE: The RTW class of 8ft-wide Leyland Titan PD2s were late appearing in the Croydon area, and then only for a short period in the mid-1960s from Brixton garage on the 95, 95A and 109. RTW 170 pulls away from the stop opposite Thornton Heath garage in February 1966 on its way from the Embankment to Purley. One assumes that the Ford Prefect saloon had sufficient power to stay in front.

OPPOSITE ABOVE: Far outnumbered by AEC RTs, Leylands were always considered somewhat exotic beasts by bus spotters in the Croydon area. Camberwell was one garage that favoured them, and here we see RTL 681 heading south along the London Road towards its destination at Addiscombe in August 1954. This was one of the very last buses to retain cream-painted upper-deck window surrounds. A little earlier, Camberwell had operated the underpowered SRT type for a brief period, these being prewar STL chassis carrying an RT body, and these occasionally appeared on the 59A.

OPPOSITE BELOW: A modernised Tilling ST at the Thornton Heath Pond terminus of route 59 in the late 1930s. At this stage, the pond itself still held water, admittedly pretty polluted and no longer home to the ducks who had once been inhabitants in the days when the horses slaked their thirsts there en route to Brighton. The via blind assumes that ST 839 is working the entire route between Camden Town and Chipstead Valley, but this would have happened only on Sundays; on weekdays the service north of the pond was the responsibility of the 59A.

59
Open Air
COUNTRY
MARKET BY
GREEN LINE
ALBANY ST. REGENT ST.
LAMBETH BRIDGE
STREATHAM HIGH RD
CROYDON PURLEY
Open Air
COUNTRY
MARKET BY
GREEN LINE
ST 839
GJ 2015

ABOVE: London Transport began the replacement of trams by trolleybuses in early 1936. Among the first conversions was the route from Sutton through Croydon and South Norwood up to Crystal Palace, which became trolleybus route 645. Only 23 years later, this was withdrawn on 4 March 1959, marking the beginning of the end of the world's largest trolleybus system. Prior to that date, a somewhat careworn but still basically sound B1, No 67, is at the top of Anerley Hill. The B1s were a shortened version of the standard trolleybus and had extra-powerful brakes to cope with this steep gradient.

OPPOSITE ABOVE: All-electric buses returned in the summer of 2024 to work route 157. This dates back to 1926, beginning as a feeder to the Northern Line tube terminus at Morden; in 1959 it was extended over part of trolleybus route 654 to Crystal Palace. Fresh out of the box, Ee 186, an ADL Enviro400City-bodied BYD D8UR-DD, has reached the top of Anerley Hill on 29 June 2024.

OPPOSITE BELOW: The Rev John Lines MBE's preserved Guy Arab G 351, the sole surviving wartime austerity-specification London bus, lived for a while at the end of the 1960s in the yard at Crystal Palace station, with various other vintage buses. It had been brought there following acqusition from its last owner, Burton on Trent Corporation, and is keeping company with the author's 1948-vintage Riley RMA. Today, a completely restored G 351 is based at the London Bus Museum at Brooklands, but still meeting up from time to time with the owner who achieved so much to immortalise this valuable memento of an almost forgotten era.

23

Croydon Transport

An Alexander ALX400-bodied Dennis Trident of Travel London has almost reached the summit of the steep Anerley Hill leading to the 157's Crystal Palace terminus in the spring of 2005. The top of the hill is where Croydon, London and Kent meet, while the Kent countryside extends across the distant horizon. For nearly a decade post-war, the 157 route was worked by austerity Daimlers (Ds) from Merton garage. That combination has been repeated twofold, as later Daimlers, Fleetlines also of D class, featured heavily in the 1980s, and, since 2023, Merton garage (now, of course, of Go-Ahead) has once again been in charge.

Locals relax on a June afternoon in 2024 in the grounds of Crystal Palace, accompanied by a careworn and broken statue, a remnant of the great building destroyed in the cataclysmic fire of 1936.

Croydon Transport

Heatherwick-designed and Ballymena-built, Wrightbus New Routemaster LT 711 is about to set off from the Crystal Palace terminus of route 3 and head back to central London on 29 June 2024. Such is the appeal of this unique, if now by no means latest London double-decker, that many of the type feature all-over advertising, as demonstrated to good effect by this one. Route 3 is the last surviving route connecting Crystal Palace with central London, its present West End terminus being Victoria.

Crystal Palace once possessed two railway stations. High Level seen here, with a direct passageway to the Exhibition site, closed in 1954, a good deal of its *raison d'être* having vanished after the fire of 1936, but the Low Level facility continues to do excellent business.

25

The line from Victoria tunnels under Sydenham Hill and emerges into a distinctly impressive edifice. In this 1994 photograph, taken from the steam special hauled by N Class 2-6-0 No 31874, the booking office can be seen high above, and just visible is a hint of the grand glass and iron palace that bequeathed its name to the whole area. The Ns were an R E L Maunsell design of mixed-traffic locomotive for the South Eastern and Chatham Railway and construction carried on into the post-Grouping Southern Railway.

Beneath the lofty arches of Crystal Palace station, a Southern Class 377 pauses on its way from West Croydon to Victoria in 2010. This was once the direct route from Brighton to Victoria.

The Crystal Palace itself towers over the South Met Tram terminus at the top of Anerley Hill sometime in the 1920s. The little four-wheel South Metropolitan tramcar dates from Edwardian times and compares badly with later bogie cars, although it was the trolleybus that replaced them in 1936.

ABOVE: Rather like a high-stepping schooner tacking into the wind, preserved RT 1, precursor of some 8,000 variations on the RT theme, leans into the Crystal Palace roundabout at the start of the Annual Historic Commercial Vehicle run to Brighton in 2010. RT 1 took up passenger service in 1939; its present chassis is a post-war modification, but the body, which was all that would concern your average passenger, is the real thing.

OPPOSITE ABOVE: Constructed by the Southern Railway in 1935, Norwood Junction depot (75C) replaced a number of smaller sheds in the area. Surrounded by the third rail, it catered only for freight and shunting duties. At home in this 16 June 1961 are a mix of steam locomotives of LB&SCR, origin, C2X 0-6-0s and K Class 2-6-0s, Southern Railway-built N 2-6-0s and W 2-6-4Ts, and at least one diesel shunter. On the far right of the picture, curving around the depot, is the down line from Crystal Palace to Norwood Junction, used both by suburban and inter-regional freights. The depot shut in 1964.

OPPOSITE BELOW: A mile or so to the north of Norwood Junction, an Arriva London South Alexander Dennis E40H, working the 197 from Croydon Fairfield Halls to Peckham, heads along Croydon Road, Penge, on 30 June 2024. The City of London high-rises sit on the horizon.

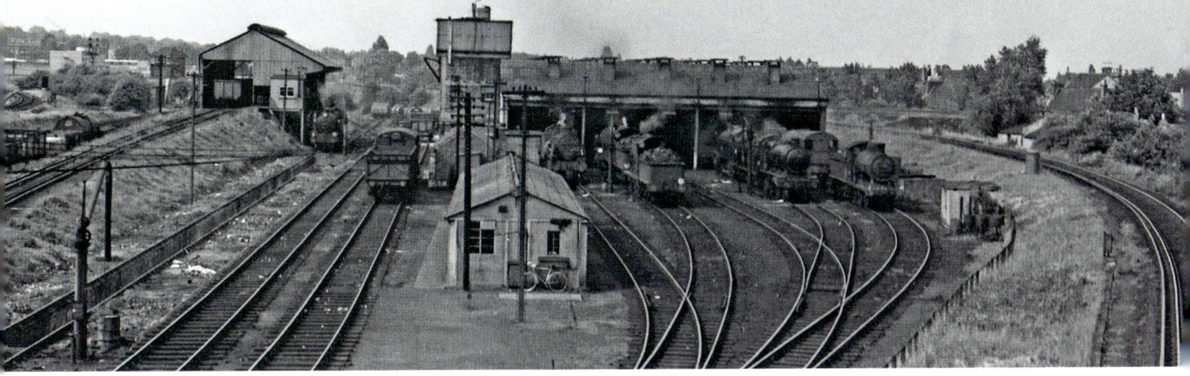

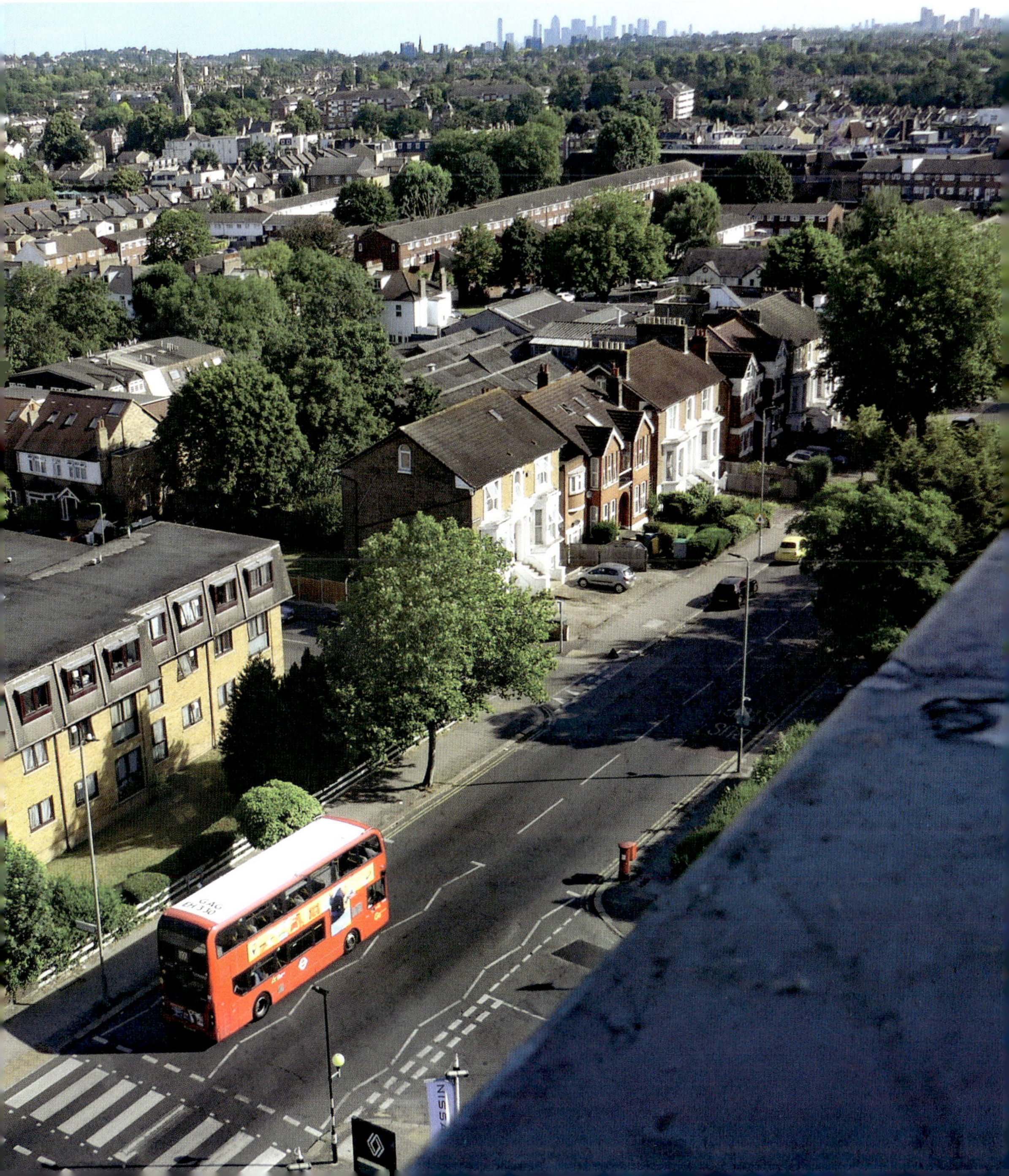

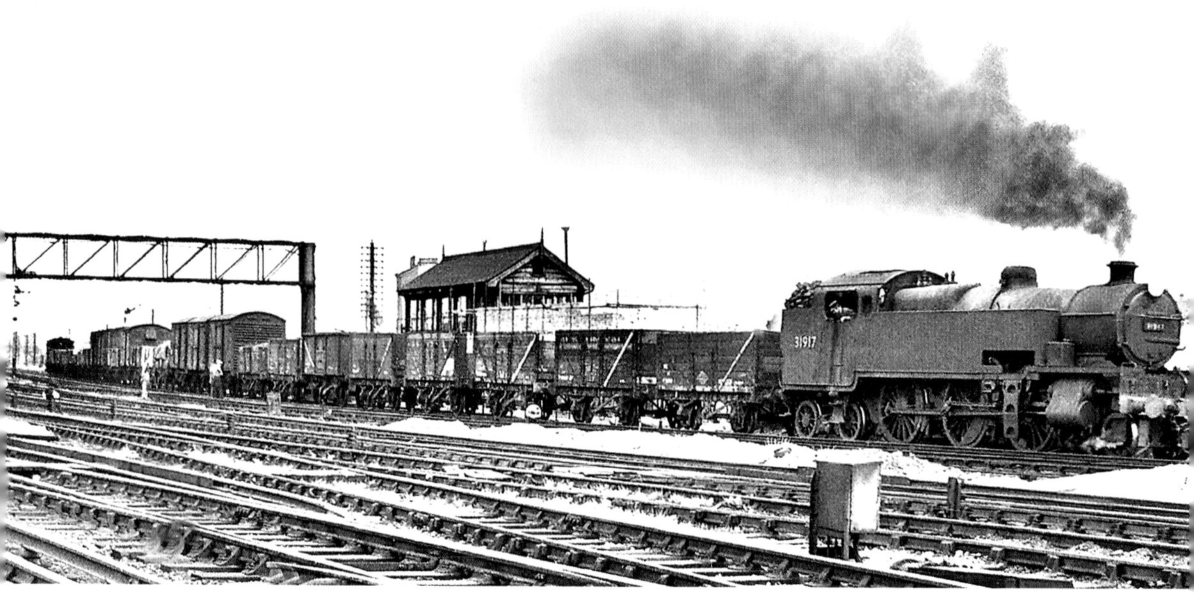
31917

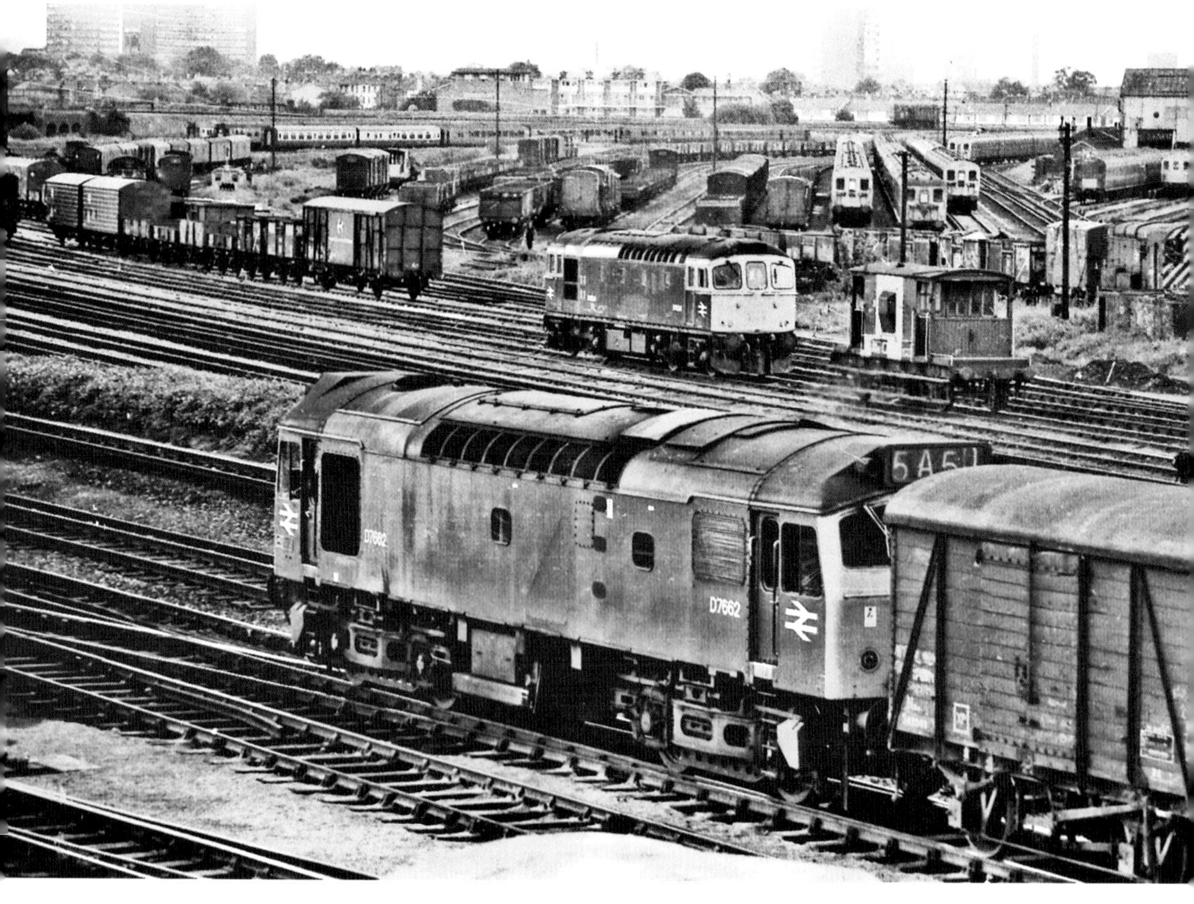
D7662

OPPOSITE ABOVE: W Class 2-6-4T No 31917 passes through Clapham Junction c1955 with a mixed freight bound for Norwood Junction, where it will continue to haul its wooden coal wagons on through West Croydon station to the power station and gas works at Purley Way. The W Class came about after the ill-fated River Class, of the same wheel arrangement, was withdrawn following a fatal accident at Sevenoaks. New frames and smaller driving wheels were constructed, and the upper works were transferred across. Otherwise confined to freight duties, the Ws could be seen on rare occasions hauling empty passenger stock.

OPPOSITE BELOW: Class 25 Co-Co No D7662 arrives at Norwood Yard in 1968 with an inter-regional freight from the London Midland Region. As can be seen, there were at that time extensive freight yards at Norwood and the adjoining Selhurst, which was the EMU depot.

BELOW: Two EPB units speed through Norwood Junction station in 1969, their next stop East Croydon. Having begun their journey at Charing Cross, the four-coach units will divide at Purley, one half going on to Tattenham Corner on the edge of Epsom Downs, the other to Caterham at the furthest fringes of suburbia. The first EPBs came out in 1951, three years after the Southern Railway was absorbed into British Railways, but these units were pure Southern Railway in concept and design. They looked very like the 4-SUBs, but there were notable differences, not least that the cabs had to be entered through the guard's compartment. The revised electrical equipment enabled faster acceleration, there were electro-pneumatic brakes and, while they couldn't couple with 4-SUBs, they could with CEPB express units.

Norwood Junction-bound Central Area ST 48 of Norwood (N) garage works a route 68A journey that has begun at Chalk Farm, c1947. The first ST-class AEC Regents arrived in late 1929, beginning passenger-carrying duties early in 1930 and served all over the London Transport system, being particularly familiar in the Croydon area. All had gone by the beginning of 1950, two of the last five working out of Norwood Garage until 25 January of that year. Just one standard ST has been preserved, Country Area ST 821, although ex-Thomas Tilling open staircase ST 922 is based at the London Bus Museum at Brooklands and is often seen out and about.

The all-Pullman trains were the best appointed in terms of comfort and prestige, if not necessarily the fastest. Two that regularly passed through the Croydon area, and this is the 'Golden Arrow', which ran between London Victoria and Dover or sometimes Folkestone, where it connected with a cross-Channel steamer, which in turn handed its privileged passengers on to the 'Fleche D'Or' to be conveyed to the Gare du Nord in Paris. On 26 May 1951, it is passing Sydenham Hill, hauled by a Merchant Navy Pacific.

With the electrification of the Brighton line in 1933, the 'Southern Belle' was renamed the 'Brighton Belle', a soubriquet that generations of attractive young Brighton ladies were pleased to adopt as their own. Adorned in full Pullman chocolate and cream livery, the train looked splendid but, perversely, British Rail repainted it blue and grey, producing an effect, to quote, 'similar to an elderly dowager adopting miniskirts'. Here the down ten-coach train takes the curve between Thornton Heath and Selhurst stations on 1 June 1971, not long before the Belle's last run took place in April 1972. I travelled in the cab once, and several times in the rather more luxuriously appointed passenger accommodation, and in both situations found the riding somewhat rough, which was a feature of all EMUs of that era. By the time of my cab ride, the schedule had been cut from one hour to 55 minutes, so that the BEL units could keep pace with the recently introduced BR-designed 4-CIG units, which, as the motorman remarked, could easily have been reduced to 45 minutes, no trouble, but 'there are a number of locations we pass where I wouldn't like to be drinking my coffee.'

4-LAV No 2943 brings up the rear of a Brighton to Victoria stopping train at Burgess Hill in the summer of 1967. Opposite in the sidings are withdrawn 6-PAN carriages, prominent among them a pantry (SR speak for buffet) car and its adjoining vehicle composed largely of First Class compartments. The 4-LAVs were designed to work slow and semi-fast trains on the Brighton line and seldom strayed from it, although they did have one early morning regular run to Eastbourne.

Croydon Transport

A one time 3-SUB EMU converted from LSWR steam-hauled carriages by the Southern Railway c1930 obtained a further lease of life and is seen here at Selhurst depot in 1968 in the role of instruction unit. Would that it had been preserved, for no example of the large number of these units that served suburban south London so well for so long remains with us. Sadly, it was broken up soon after this photograph was taken. Even so, it is tricky knowing what to do with a preserved electric multiple-unit, which is perhaps why there are so few of them.

Selhurst Southern Railway depot in 2010, seen from Selhurst station. Class 416 electric multiple-units, which are found all over the suburbs, feature, along with Class 170 diesel-electric multiple-units used on the Oxted line. The pale green unit is from a previous generation converted to departmental use.

Two Southern Class 455 EMUs, dating from 1982–85, negotiate the Selhurst Triangle in 2015. In the background are the ever-growing high-rise buildings of central Croydon. The Triangle is where trains from East and West Croydon meet and make their way to or from the Selhurst and Norwood Junction directions by either fast or slow tracks. There were serious proposals for an extensive rebuild to relieve the pressure on East Croydon, but these were quashed by the government in 2021. With the emphasis on home working and the general run-down in the appeal of central Croydon, there is little likelihood of progress.

No 85, a short-wheelbase B1 trolleybus of 1936, is near the end of its days in 1958, heading through Selhurst on its way from Crystal Palace to Croydon, Carshalton and Sutton. The long shadow of the pole supporting the overhead wiring suggests that this is a winter evening picture. Brumfit & Bailey are no longer in business.

ABOVE: A train of southbound 2-BILs and 2-HALs for the Mid-Sussex route passes the Selhurst Triangle in 1968. The BILs dated from the Eastbourne electrification of the mid-1930s. Each unit consisted of a Second Class motor and a composite driving trailer, with corridors within each carriage and lavatories but no corridor connections. Visually, they matched the main-line express stock both inside and out, and were very up to date. The guard's and luggage compartment had a floor space of 60 square feet, reflecting the fact that there was relatively more luggage carried per passenger back in the 1930s than by the time this photograph was taken. The 2-HALs, although intended for similar duties, did not come out until 1939, by which time Oliver Bulleid was in charge of design. Bulleid had some very odd ideas and the HALs were generally regarded as the least pleasing EMUs ever to be placed before the public; on entering, passengers tended to take it all in and enquire when the interiors might be completed. Though these were intended for the Medway electrification scheme, after the war the operating authorities made no distinction between a BIL and a HAL.

OPPOSITE ABOVE: No 377137, an EMU that today is at home on both London-area suburban duties and express coast work, approaches the up slow line platform at Selhurst station, c2014.

OPPOSITE BELOW: A powerful, brand new Hugh Dynes recovery vehicle, seen from the upper deck of a Volvo B9TL at work on Superloop SL7 at Waddon in April 2024. It is able to cope with any heavy-duty casualty; a 44-tonne artic and trailer, for example, so a double-deck bus poses no problem.

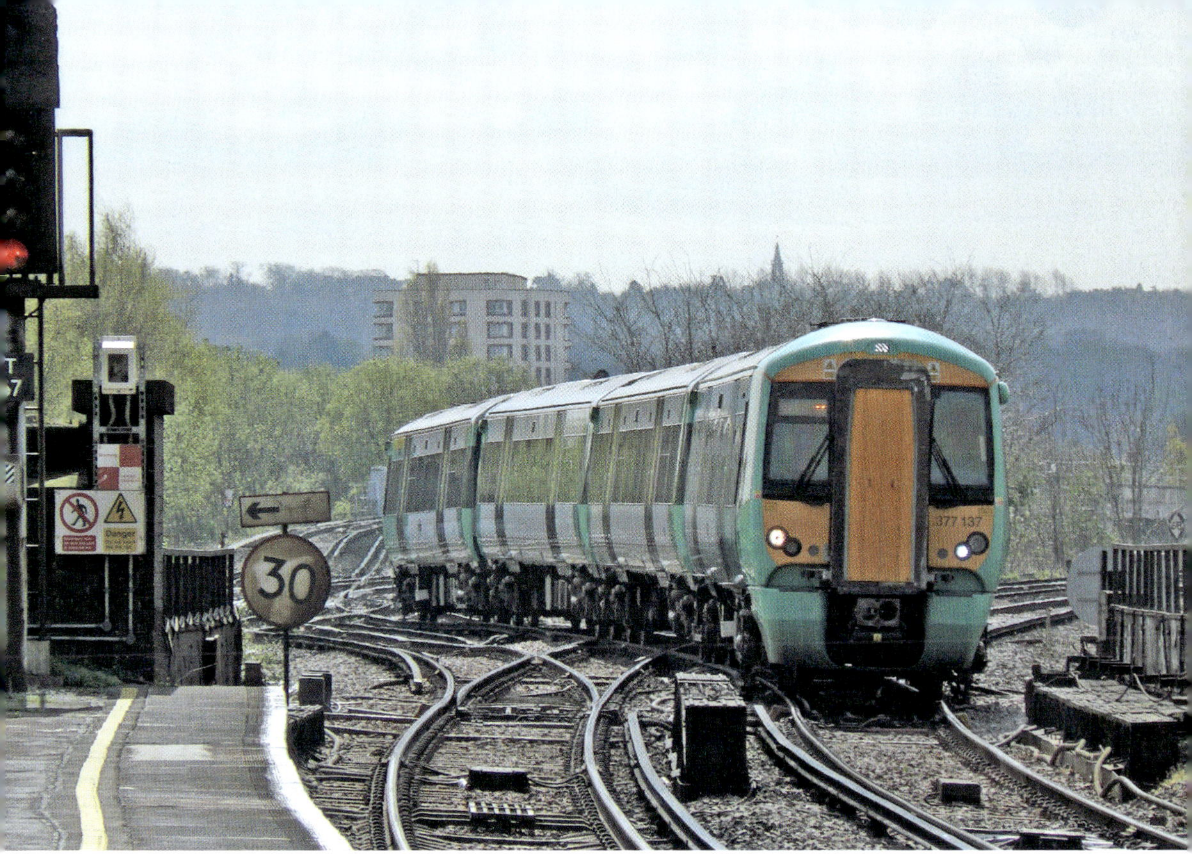
30
377 137

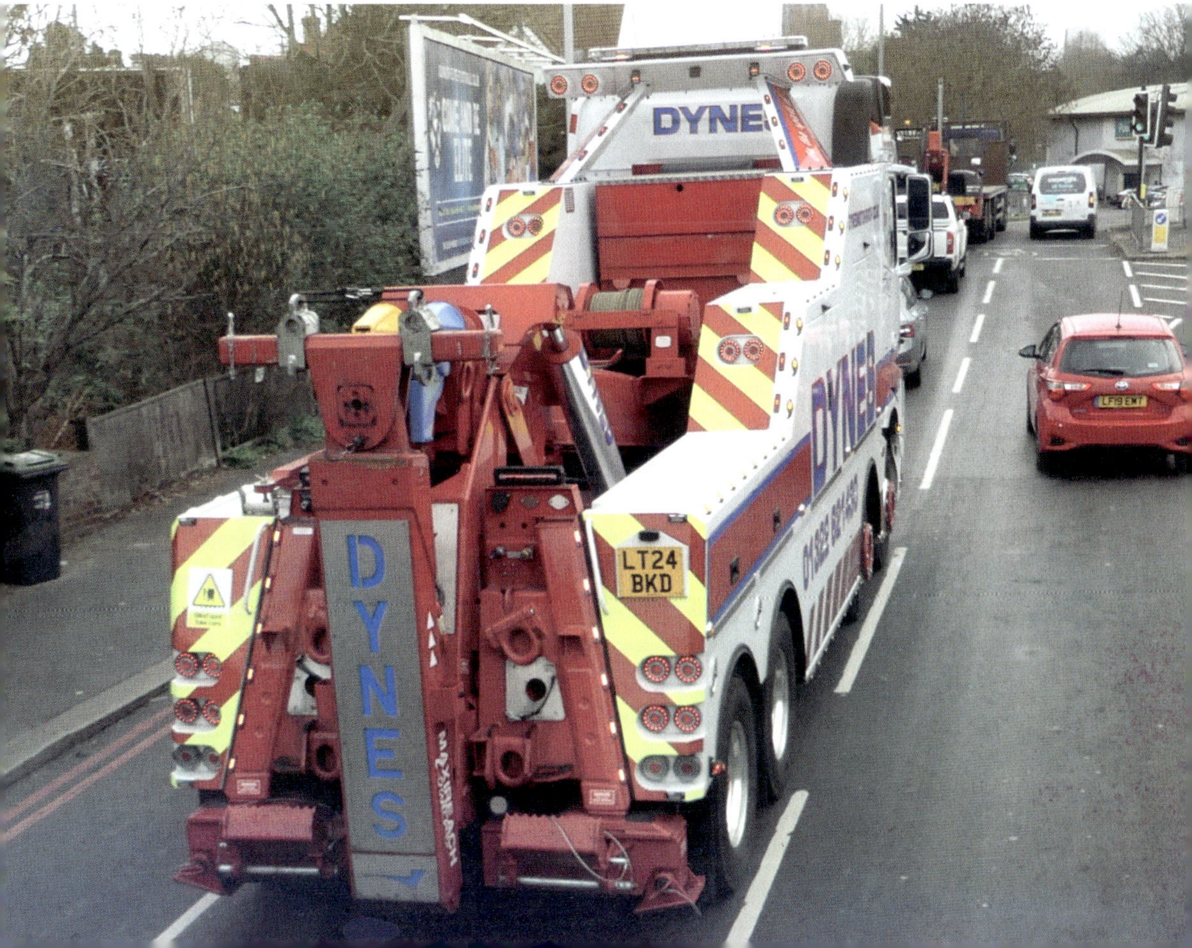
DYNES
LT24
BKD
DYNES
LF19 EWT

A scene of dereliction at Croydon Power Station, 6 April 1971. The works had its own, quite extensive railway system. Seen here, their work finished but still intact, are an English Electric locomotive dating from 1924 and a Bagnall saddle tank dating from 1946.

Waddon Marsh station, c1955 with a West Croydon to Wimbledon '2' train departing. All around is the huge power station premises that employed both steam and electric shunting locomotives to work its extensive sidings. Superficially, the entire Southern Electric system might have appeared to be one vast monolith; it did claim to be the largest suburban electric system in the world. But the West Croydon to Wimbledon line was like no other. Firstly, it was mostly single-track; secondly, much of its surroundings were semi-rural, despite being deep in suburbia. Thirdly, it needed only two units to work it, although there were actually four, which were converted from steam stock and were partly corridor, and finally, it took just 18 minutes to travel from one end of the line to the other.

Crompton diesel-electric locomotive No D6512 has just brought in a coal train for Croydon Power Station in 1969. In the background, a Peckett 0-6-0ST can be seen shunting coal wagons. Officially diesels had taken over this work – you can just see the corner of one – but steam was still called upon in an emergency, making this the last normal steam working anywhere on Croydon's extensive rail network. D6512 is standing next to the track of the electrified West Croydon to Wimbledon branch line.

ABOVE: A close-up view of the Peckett. This was one of three built by the Bristol-based firm in 1948 especially to work at the power station, known as Croydon B, which opened in 1950. Withdrawn shortly after this photograph was taken, the Peckett passed into preservation. Croydon B closed in 1980 and all that survives are two of its chimneys, kept as features by IKEA, which now occupies the site.

OPPOSITE ABOVE: From almost the same location as the picture on page 38, tram No 2533 sets off from Waddon Marsh on its way to Wimbledon in 2007. The view is dominated by the two chimneys reminding us of the long-vanished Croydon B power station. The West Croydon to Wimbledon line ceased operating as part of the main line rail network in June 1997, and on 10 May 2000, the first tram to enter public service in the Croydon area since 1951 took up work.

OPPOSITE BELOW: A good deal of street running was planned for Tramlink right from the start. In the heart of Croydon, it is now perfectly possible to sit in a George Street open-air café and watch the trams go by, in the exact spot where they once did between 1902 and 1927. In this July 2002 scene, tram No 2543 is about to pass the Tudor almshouses, by far the oldest buildings in Croydon town centre.

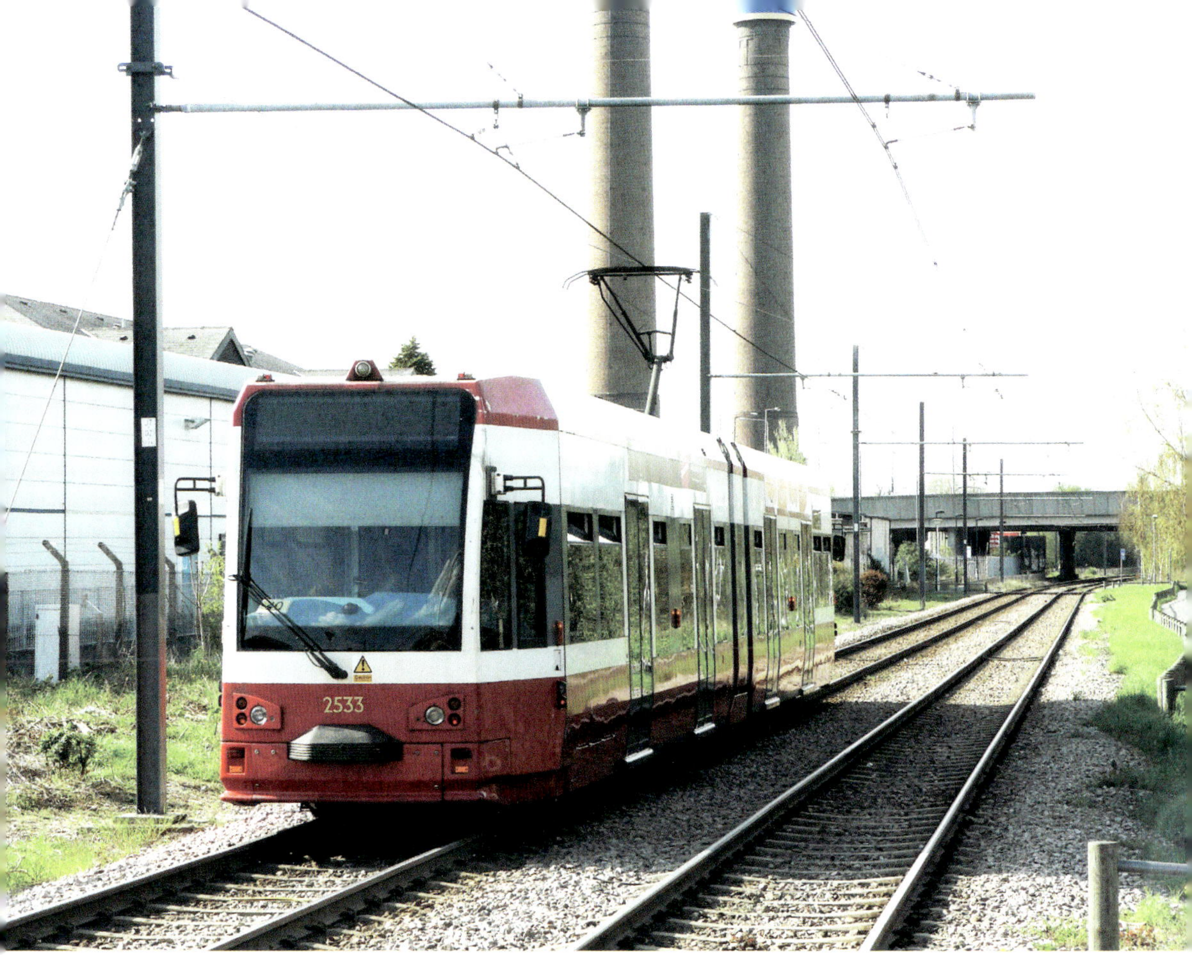

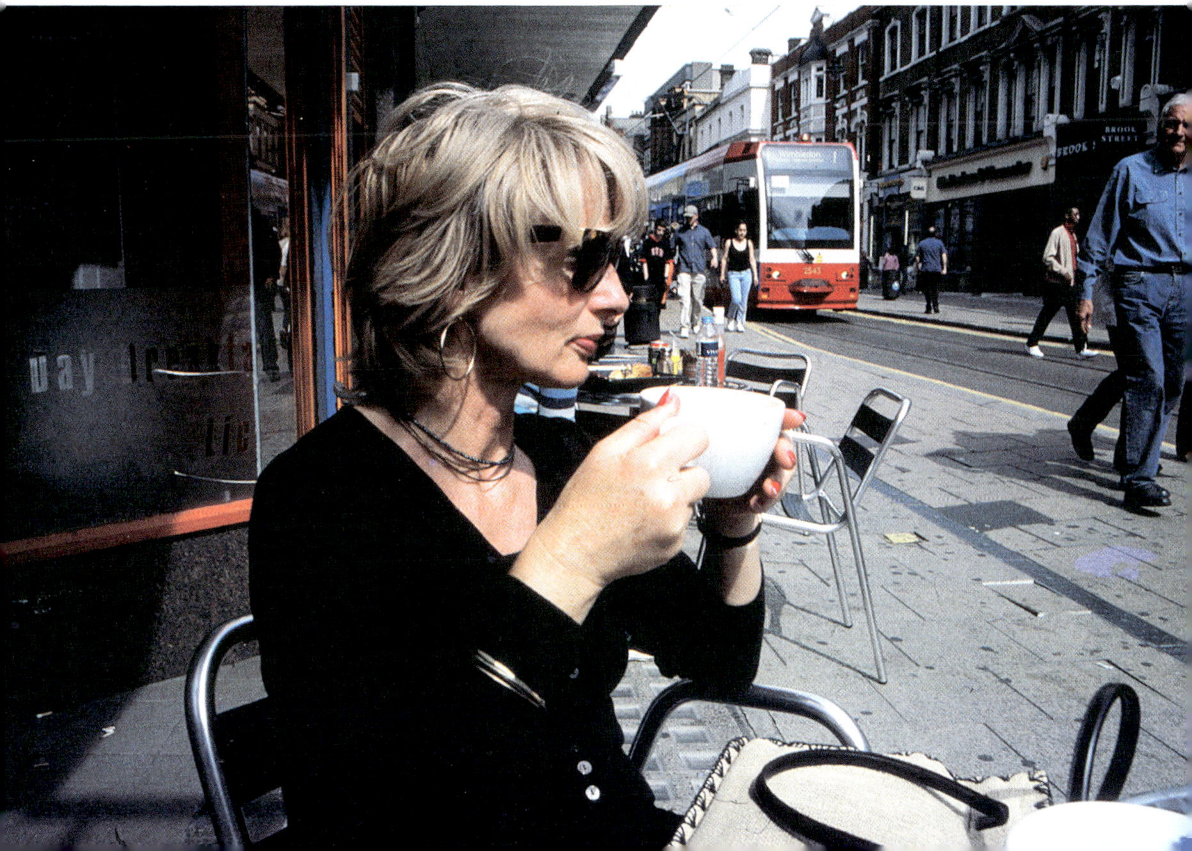

So successful was Tramlink that more trams had to be ordered, 12 Stadler Variobahns arriving in 2012 and 2016. No 2557 is seen at West Croydon bus and tram station in the summer of 2023. In the distance is a No 250 bus bound for Brixton via much of the route once worked by the 16 and 18 trams. Sadly, by no means all of central Croydon is blessed with such flower displays.

Original tram No 2540 waits for the lights so it can swing across Park Lane and take up the inside lane on the approach to George Street during January 2001.

London Country RT 604 of Chelsham garage heads along Park Lane on a warm summer day in 1978 towards its West Croydon terminus, its blind already turned for the journey back to Warlingham. In the distance is a Godstone RML on the 409. Now preserved, RT 604 was once the oldest working bus on the entire NBC network and ended its career shortly after as London Country's last RT.

Park Lane in August 2023, with Stagecoach Alexander Dennis E40D No 11063 from Catford garage on route 75 ahead of a Metrobus Volvo B9TL on route 403, which has for many years been a red bus route.

Metrobus Volvo Olympian No 849, working the 119 from Bromley North, is about to turn out of George Street into Park Lane, while a tram heads in the opposite direction, February, 2001.

South Croydon, looking north in 2007. Judging by the greenery, someone seems to be caring for this well-used junction station. On the far left is a Thameslink Class 315 heading for Bedford, while on the right a Southern Class 455 heads towards Purley.

Amid high-rise buildings, a Victoria-bound class 377 approaches East Croydon on 8 June 2024.

A Mid-Sussex line train composed of 2-BILs and 2-HALs, with 2-BIL No. 2095 leading, passes South Croydon in 1968.

The pioneer ST 1 bound for South Croydon, c1947.

The last RT route to be operated by Croydon garage was the 197. Newly overhauled RT 538 is seen inside the garage in May 1972.

RT 1868 of Thornton Heath garage is adding nicely to London Transport's bank balance with almost all seats taken, many by schoolboys, one Friday afternoon in the summer of 1970 by the Swan and Sugar Loaf at South Croydon.

ABOVE: A Victoria to Portsmouth express, with 4-COR unit No 3140 leading, passing beneath a bank of semaphore signals between East and South Croydon, c1948.

OPPOSITE ABOVE: East Croydon in the summer of 2023 with a Gatwick Express, which will not be stopping, heading through platform 3. The leading unit, No 387227, is a variation on the Electrostar theme represented by the 377 unit departing platform 1 for Victoria, and both were built at the Litchurch Lane works in Derby. Over on the next platform is an earlier 455 suburban unit dating from 1987. Beyond are the wooded heights of Upper Norwood and Sydenham, or, since the arrival of the wondrous iron and glass extravaganza from Hyde Park in the 1850s, better known worldwide as Crystal Palace.

OPPOSITE BELOW: The 12-coach Newhaven Boat Train heads through East Croydon, hauled by H2 Atlantic No 2425 *Trevose Head, c*1939. Quite often, at least one Pullman car was included in this service, although there doesn't appear to be one on this occasion. The Brighton Atlantics were long associated with this train and, although one or other of the three Southern main line electric locomotives was normally employed post-war, the 4-4-2s still made appearances throughout the 1950s.

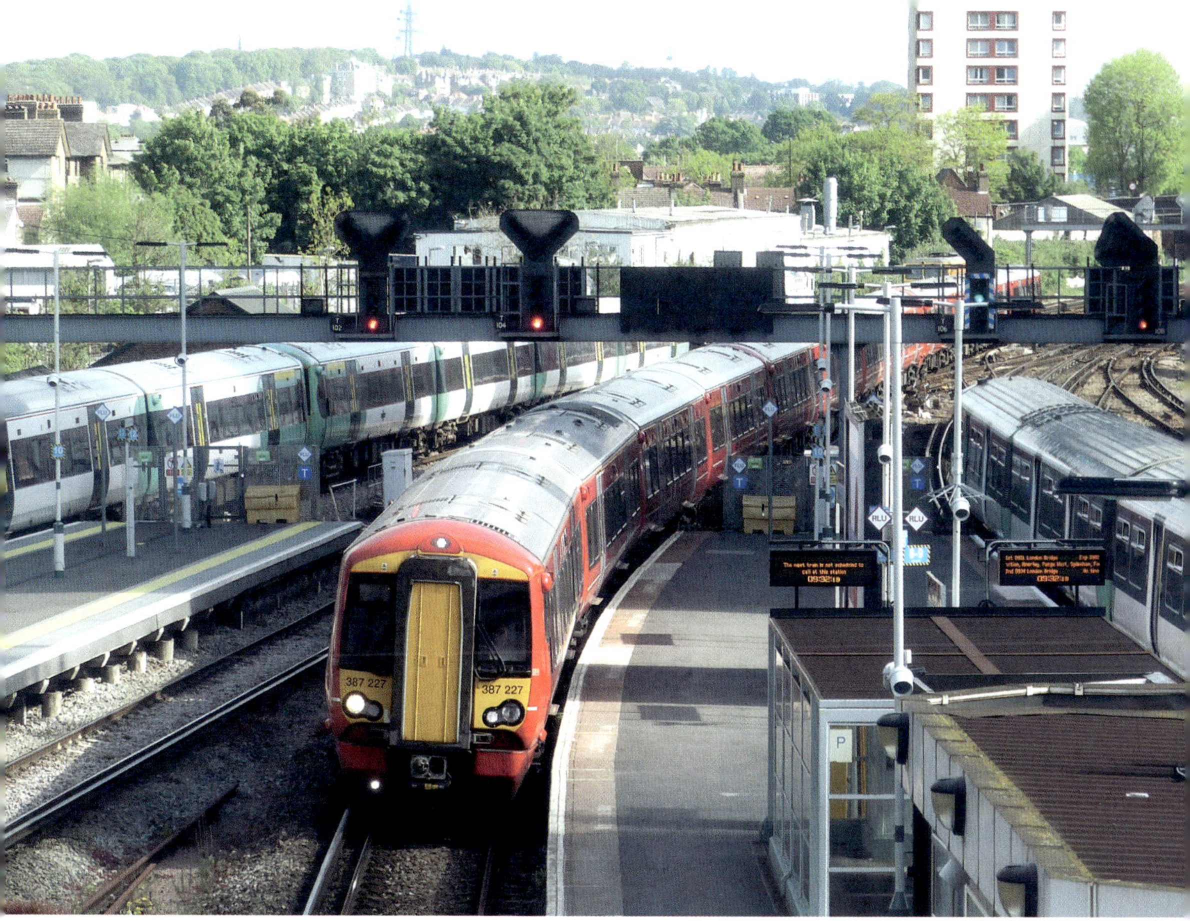
387 227
387 227

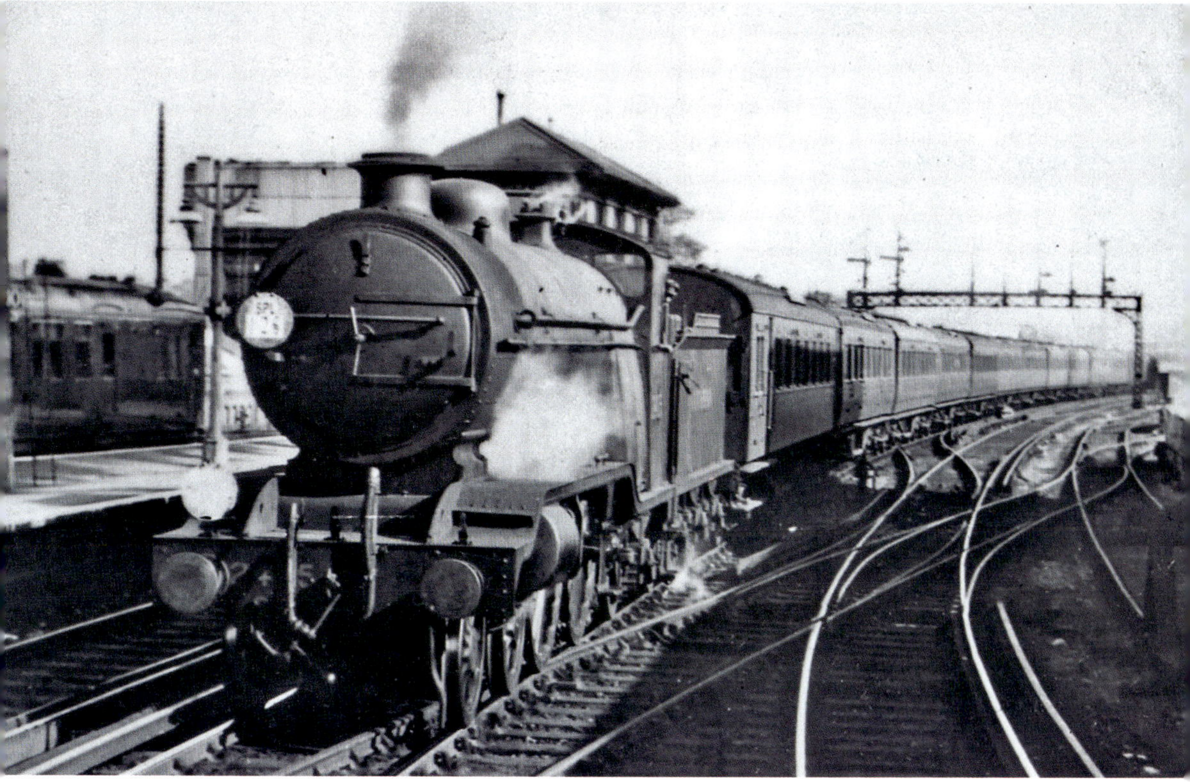

ABOVE: Though it is still possible to travel through East Croydon on a train heading for Newhaven and make connections to the continent, in a sense the modern equivalent is the Gatwick Express. Gatwick Airport originated before World War Two but by the 1950s it had grown to become London's second most important airport and, over the years, a variety of solutions have been tried to maintain a frequent, fast connection with London Victoria. Here, one of the most stylish, a contrast to the generations of basically flat-fronted EMUs, is seen passing East Croydon in 2005.

OPPOSITE ABOVE: At East Croydon on Sunday 17 March 2024 (St Patrick's Day), a Victoria to Brighton train is about to depart. Staff and passengers mingle and, just possibly, get in each other's way. Above towers 'Little Manhattan'.

OPPOSITE BELOW: 1882-vintage SE&CR O1 0-6-0 No 31048 is on station pilot duties at East Croydon on 13 May 1959.

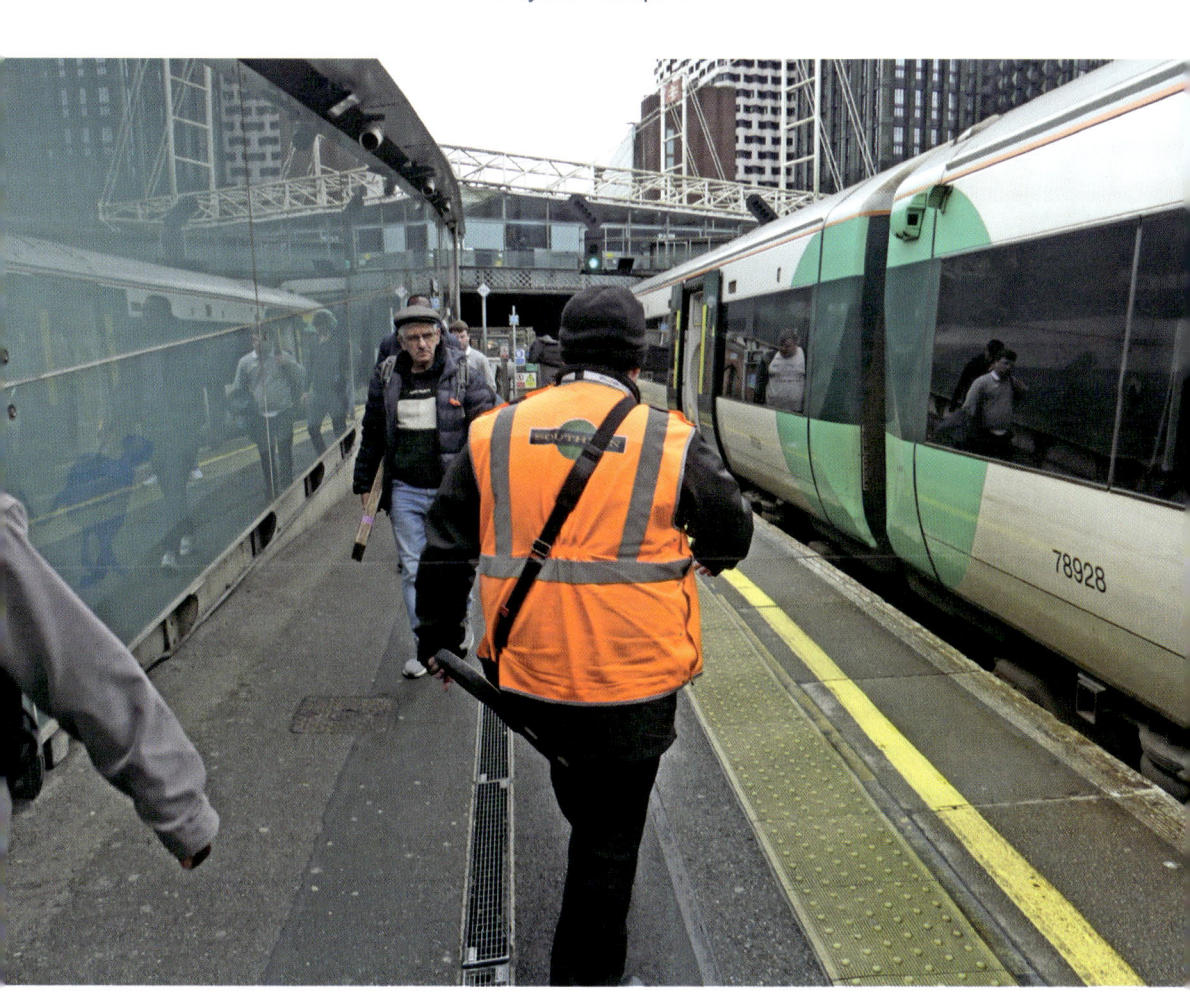

Croydon Transport

TOP: One of the O1 class has been preserved and is seen here in all its pre-grouping glory working on the Swanage Railway in April 2024, coupled to LSWR No 563 4-4-0 of 1893.

ABOVE: Purley, c1950. A view from the upper deck of a bus awaiting a green light so it can head towards Croydon, possibly overtaking the Feltham. This is the number 16/18 terminus, the furthest south London trams have ever reached, so far.

OPPOSITE ABOVE: Looking south at Purley on a wet day, 9 June 2024.

OPPOSITE BELOW: An identical, albeit lower-deck view from preserved London Country RT 604, about to head over the crossroads towards Croydon in 2017. An Abellio E20D single-decker has just come down the hill on the A23, past the site of Croydon Aerodrome.

Croydon Transport

ABOVE: The Purley High Street terminus of Londonlinks Leyland Lynx-operated route 289 in May 1997. The Lynx was the last pure Leyland single-deck bus design and was a fairly rare beast in the London area.

OPPOSITE ABOVE: An example of an older generation of single-deckers is LT 1149, seen parked outside Croydon garage, c1948. Just visible in the background is an all-Leyland PD1 of STD class.

OPPOSITE BELOW: Not easily missed, the Purley station yard depot of London Concrete. This is one of 110 such depots served by rail in the United Kingdom.

SOUTH CROYDON
234
VIA
PURLEY
GP 3457

0671
PURLEY
LONDON
CONCRETE

TOP: A Purley-bound train of stone wagons passes the Kennet and Avon Canal at Crofton in 2024.

ABOVE: Coulsdon North sidings with, on the left, a train of LB&SCR overhead electric stock and, on the right, a train of third-rail stock converted from former LSWR steam-hauled stock. At this time, First Class was still provided in just about all suburban trains. The last overhead electrics were replaced by third-rail units in September 1929, which must be when this carefully posed photograph was taken.

OPPOSITE ABOVE: An N Class 2-6-0 struggles through Coulsdon on the down slow line in deep snow in January 1955 with a Three Bridges-bound goods train.

OPPOSITE BELOW: Trains pass in a sudden snowstorm at Coulsdon on 6 April 2008. On the far left is a Victoria-bound Gatwick Express while heading south is a 377 on the fast line. Discernible in the far distance are the headlights of a down slow train.

57

By the 1950s, the remaining Brighton Atlantics were in semi-retirement in the winter months but would emerge in December to help out with Christmas parcels, a task which in those days needed hundreds of extra workers, both on the Post Office and British Railways. No 32424 *Beachy Head* is passing Coulsdon North on a bitterly cold 19 December 1954.

4-SUB unit No 4332 stands ready at Coulsdon North to depart for Victoria in February 1955. While nearly all the early Southern Railway suburban EMUs were converted steam-hauled stock, 55 were built new in 1925/26 and this is one of them. All were augmented post-war with an all-steel ten-compartment trailer.

They served their purpose admirably. One motor coach from a pointed-nosed example, intended for the ex-LSWR routes but later used all over the system, has been preserved and is seen at the National Railway Museum at York.

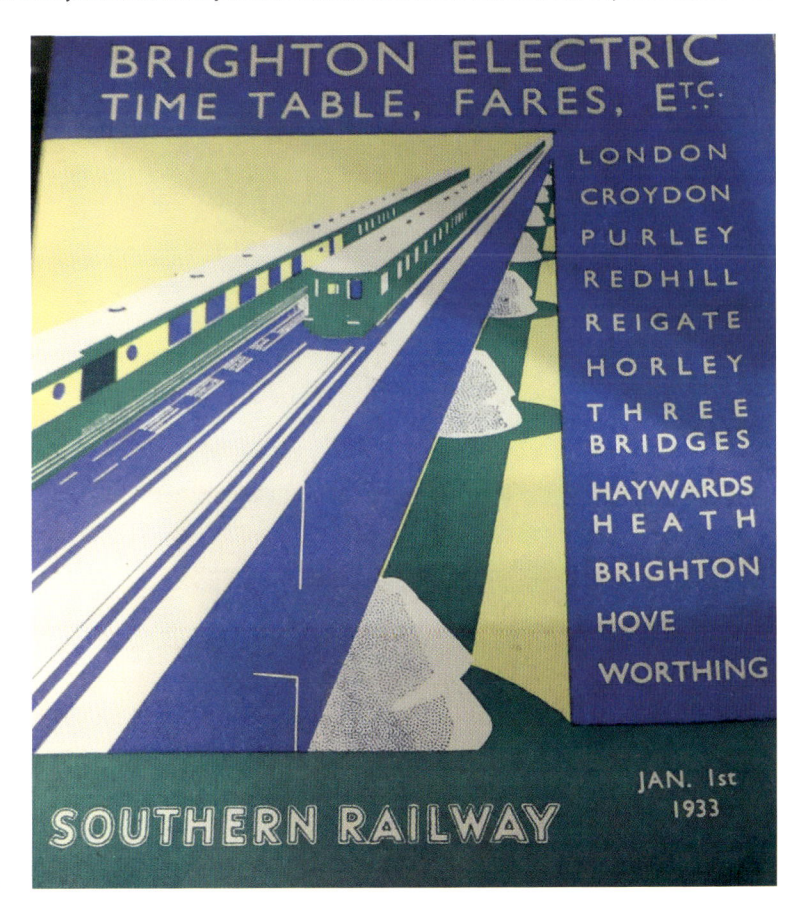

Main-line electrification came in 1933 from Victoria and London Bridge through East Croydon to Brighton, Worthing and Littlehampton, and in the summer of 1935 to Eastbourne and Hastings.

ABOVE: 23 six-coach units, each graced with a Pullman car, were provided in 1933 and 17 similar examples, but with a pantry car instead of a Pullman, followed in 1935. Three are seen at London Bridge in 1935.

OPPOSITE ABOVE: In the late 1960s, otherwise at the end of their stalwart careers, a number of the units were reformed as 6-CORs, without pantry or Pullman cars, and sent to work on the Kent Coast route. One such unit, No 3045, is seen in Selhurst depot in late 1968. To the best of my knowledge, it was the only one to be repainted with an all-yellow face, which rather suited it. I suspect it had made its last revenue-earning journey and was about to be sent on its final run to the breakers.

OPPOSITE MIDDLE: Main-line stopping and semi-fast duties were virtually monopolised, at least in their early days, on the Brighton line by 31 four-coach LAV units. They outlasted the PULs and PANs by a couple of years. One is seen in 1969 on its way from London Bridge to Reigate and Brighton, approaching South Croydon station. Two 4-EPB units are heading in the opposite direction while an RT on route 64 passes overhead.

OPPOSITE BELOW: Reigate garage was, for a time in the 1950s, the home of London Transport's collection of vintage vehicles. Included in the picture are a Q-type bus (the type also worked as Green Line coaches), an early T-type coach and, partly visible, a TF coach and an E1 tram.

3045

REDHILL
EARLSWOOD STN
447 MEADVALE
REIGATE
LONDON TRANSPORT
BXD 576
REIGATE
GREEN LINE
T219
GK 5486

Croydon could at one time boast two coach companies. Bourne & Balmer was one of them, a long-established firm that was eventually absorbed by Timpsons in the 1960s. This is a 1934-vintage Dennis.

Equally well known was John Bennett, which used to pick up its passengers down a side street off the London Road at West Croydon. It owned a very long-lived fleet of elderly early-1930s Leyland Tiger coaches that it had rebodied post-war so that they lasted until the late 1950s.

In the late 1960s there was still employment for a number of 08 shunters in the Norwood freight yards, as seen here in 1968.

Norwood Junction passenger, 2022.

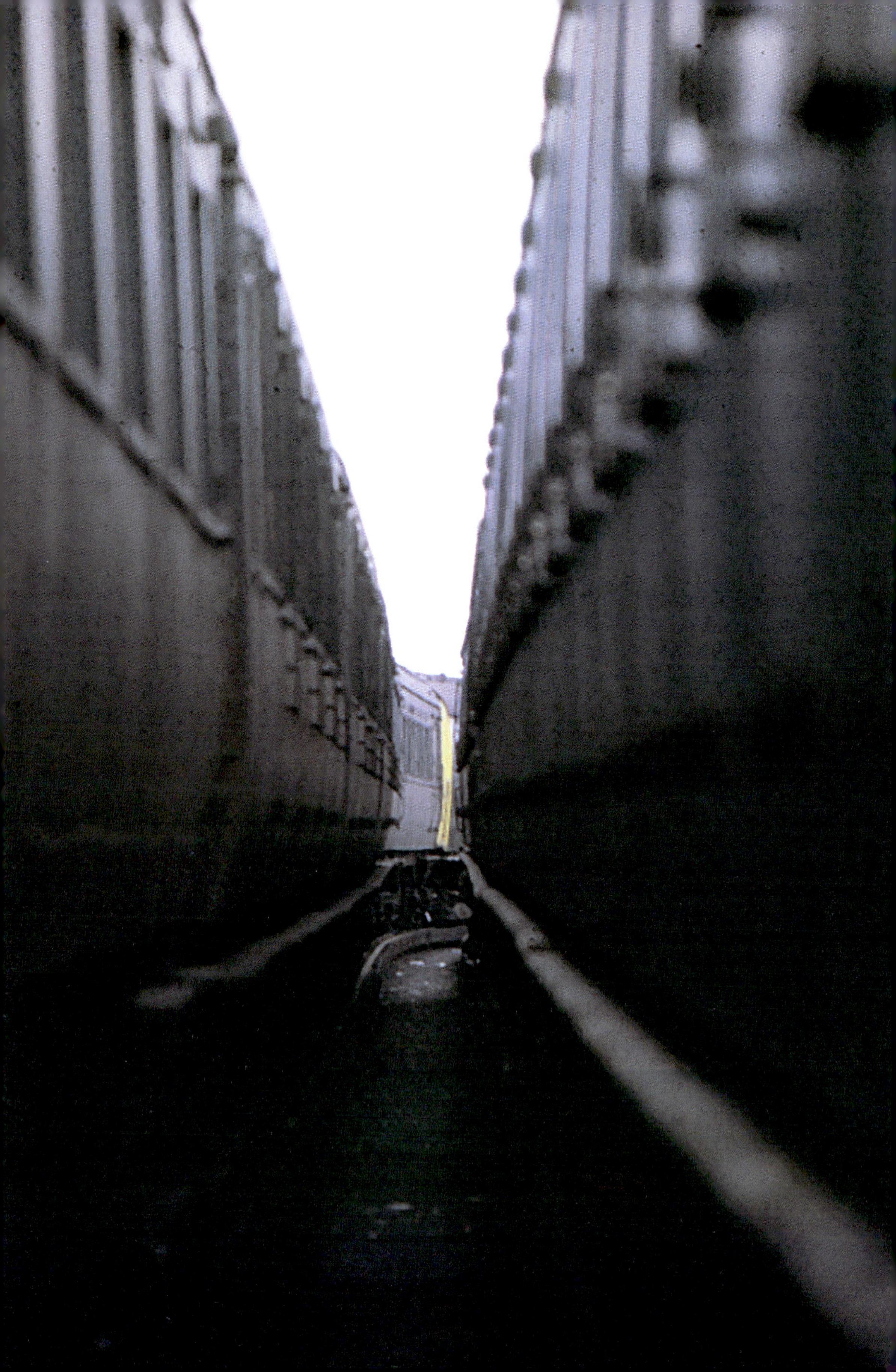

ABOVE: In 2023/24, a complete ring of Superloop express bus services circling the suburbs was set up. The SL7 runs between Heathrow Airport and West Croydon, taking over from the X26. Wrightbus-bodied Volvo B9TL WVL 486 of Metrobus is seen passing along Broad Street, Teddington, in March 2024.

OPPOSITE: Selhurst depot in 1968, looking between a 4-EPB on the right and a 6-COR on the left.

The most attractive of all the many and varied liveries worn by the companies that succeeded London Country was that of London & Country, operating in the south-western quadrant of the old Country Area. A number of its buses passed in 1995 to Londonlinks, a short-lived concern pre-dating the all-encompassing Arriva. In this picture taken in the same year, Volvo Olympian No 690 is seen at West Croydon, about to commence work on the 403, once again – albeit briefly – a green route.

Tram No 2546 in the modern livery of this undertaking crosses the London Road at West Croydon in March 2024, on its way to New Addington.

West Croydon in 1960. From right to left are RT 4679 of Catford garage and two Country Area buses, RTs 3124 and 3140, both of Godstone.

On 4 March 1959, motor buses replaced the 654 trolleybus route between Sutton and Crystal Palace. A number of newly overhauled RTs, the majority with roofbox bodies, took over, and here in Carshalton on that inaugural day is RT 181, beneath the not yet removed overhead wires,.

RM 1000 was the one-thousandth Routemaster and dated from 1961. For a time, it was Croydon garage's showbus, and in the summer of 1982 is seen passing Broad Green on its way to West Croydon in immaculate, sparkling condition.

Further along the London Road, in 1973, RT 1191 has arrived at West Croydon while working the 109, the premier trunk route through Croydon. In those days it linked the Embankment with Purley.

All-Leyland K1 trolleybus No 1078 takes advantage of the long stretch of Mitcham Common with no bus stops but plenty of grass, to speed northwards, c1960.

ABOVE: In May 2002, an Elmers End-bound tram has just departed Mitcham Junction station and is crossing the tracks of the Southern line to Sutton and Horsham.

OPPOSITE ABOVE: A Wimbledon to West Croydon former LB&SCR two-coach train pauses at Mitcham station, c1952.

OPPOSITE BELOW: Autumn in suburbia. On 17 November 2013, a Wimbledon-bound tram has just crossed the River Wandle, its next stop Morden Road.

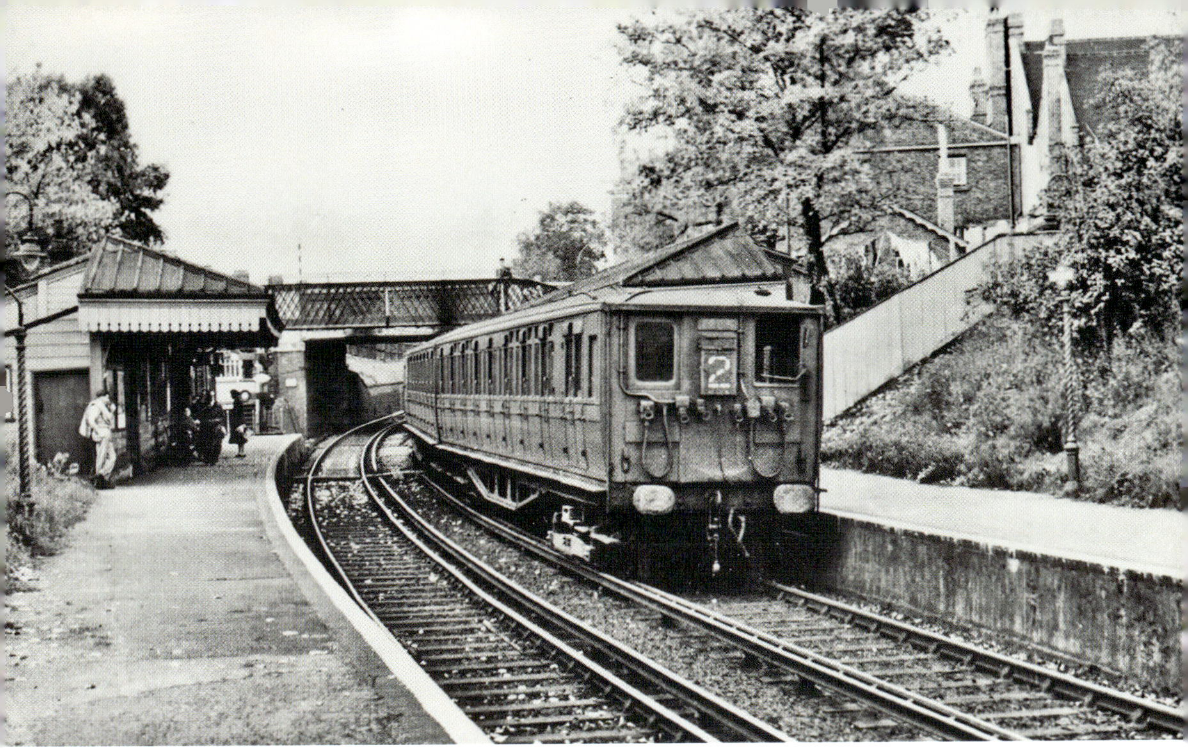
2

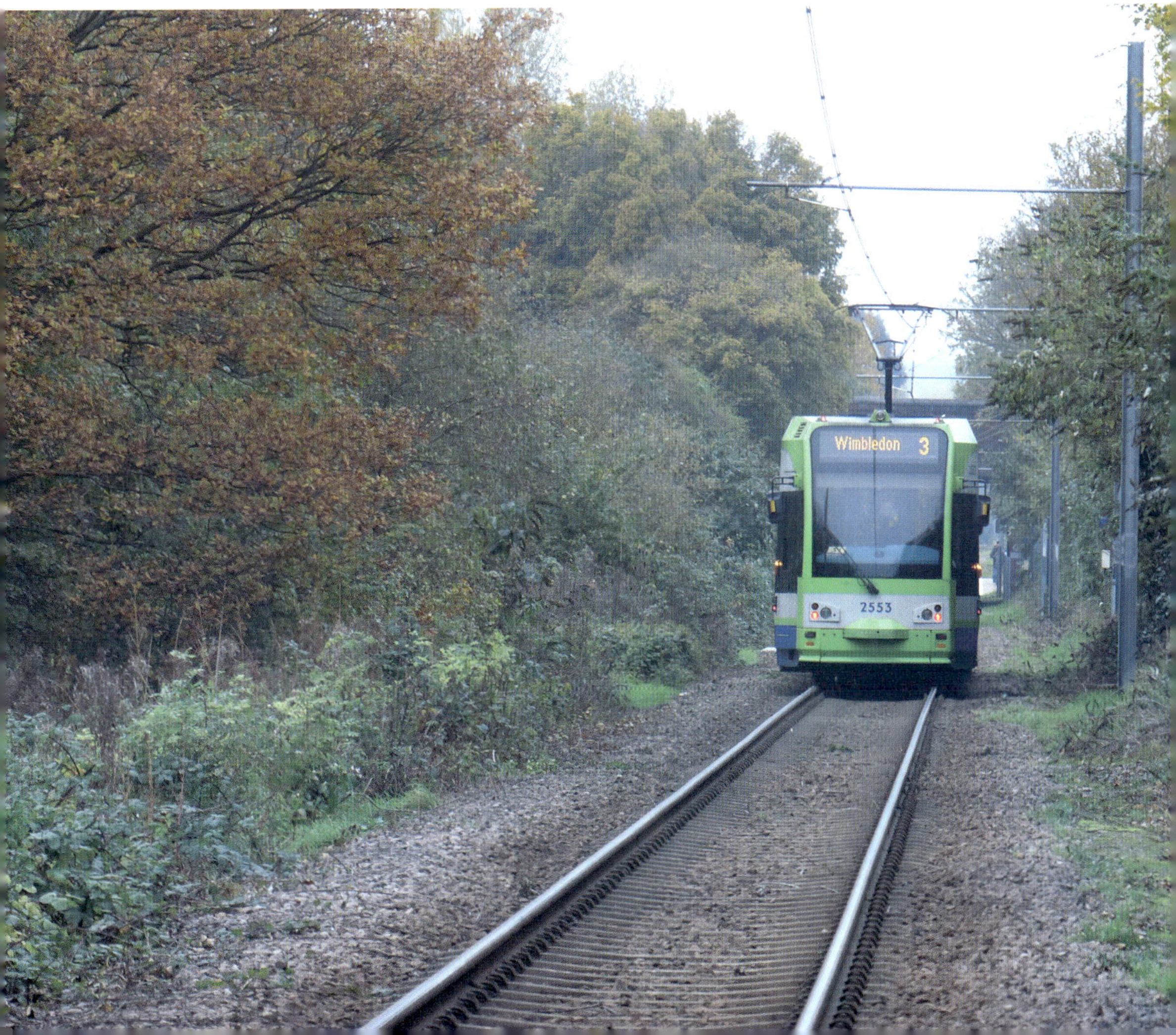
Wimbledon 3
2553

Croydon Transport

Morden depot in 1973. The tram in the previous picture is more or less directly above the Northern Line from Edgware, which terminates a few hundred yards beyond.

From 1996 to 2001, Connex South Central ran the Wimbledon to West Croydon line. In this 1997 shot, the guard of two-coach unit No 456024 at Wimbledon checks that the destination is correct.

Croydon Transport

Long before the days of Tramlink, London Transport Daimler Fleetline DMS 238 stands at the Addington terminus of route 64 whilst in the background is an RML on the 130. Fleetlines would come to the 130 group in 1975, but in this case, examples of the crew-operated DM variant.

The very last STL to work out of Croydon garage, STL 1548, is at South Park Hill Road, South Croydon, on 29 July 1953, on its way from West Croydon to Addington. Note the full destination display.

A Victoria to Bognor Regis train of HALs and BILs, by way of the Mid-Sussex line, heads south from South Croydon in 1968, 2-BIL No 2057 bringing up the rear. Just easing itself into the picture is a Selsdon-bound RT on route 54.

The 7.49 Tunbridge Wells West and Oxted to London Bridge was a City businessmen's train, consisting of a set of Bulleid corridors full of *Daily Telegraph* readers. On the approaches to South Croydon on 3 April 1958, standard 4MT 2-6-4T No 80018 is in charge.

3H DEMU No 1109 climbs the steep gradient from South Croydon through the disused platforms of Selsdon station with an Oxted line train in 1973. The upward growth of high-rise central Croydon is already evident. In contrast, the gas-lit station lights were said to be the last such survivors in the London area.

One of Bulleid's original wartime 4-SUBs, nicknamed 'Shebas' on account, to quote the Bible (1 Kings 10), of being a 'very great train', about to depart South Croydon in 1969 for Victoria.

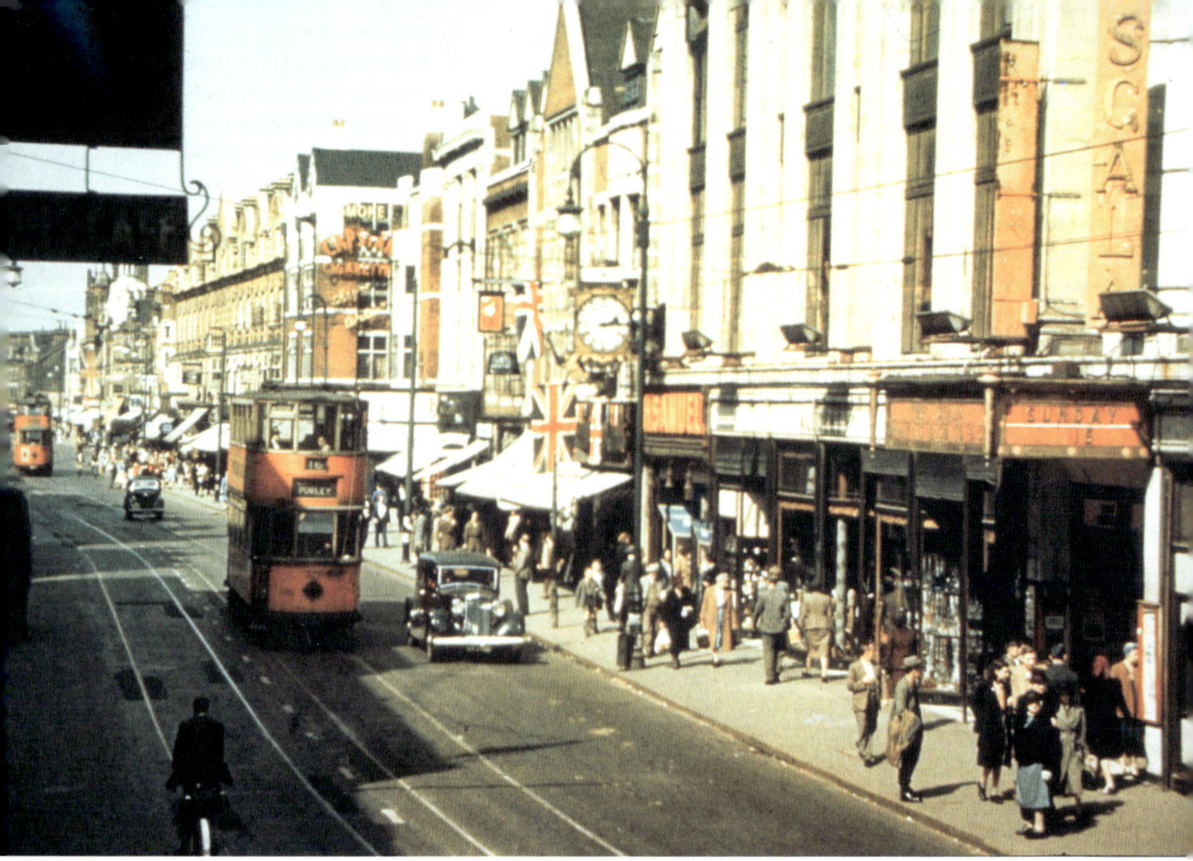
SUNDAY

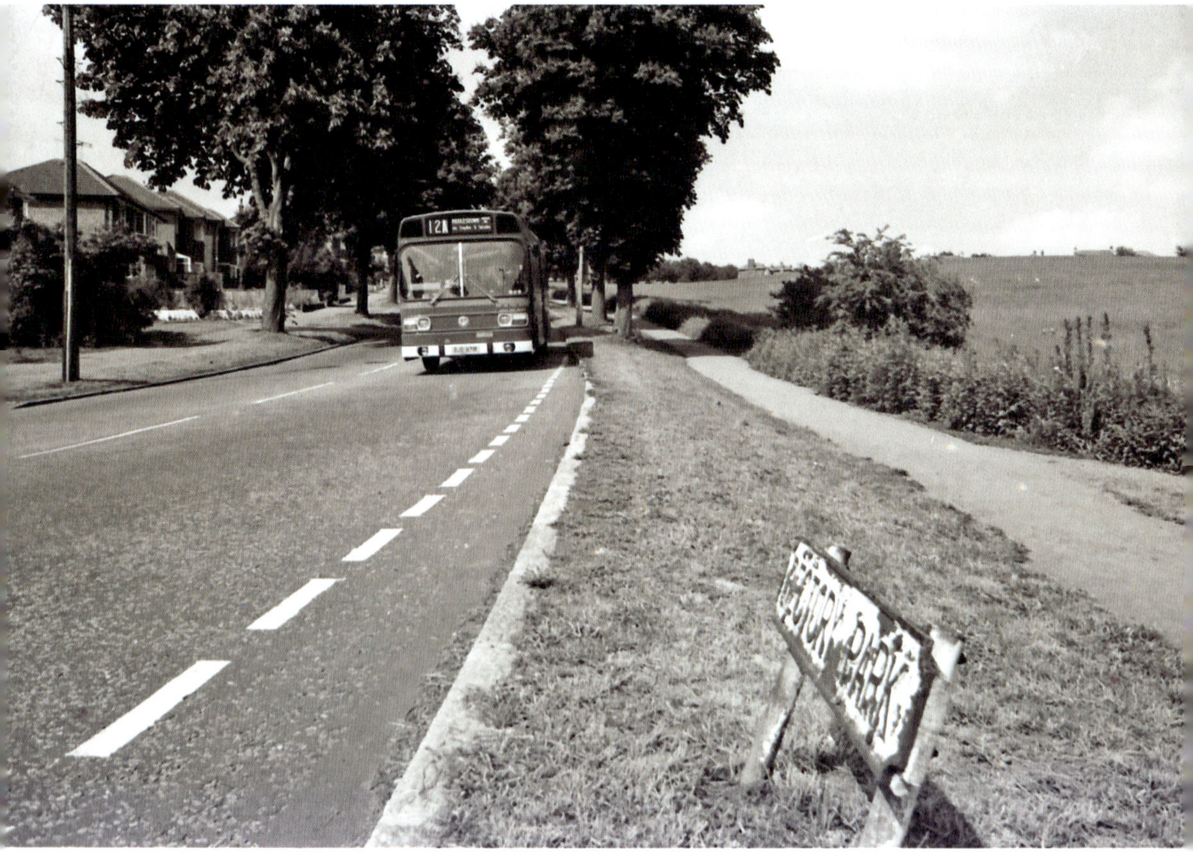
12A

Croydon Transport

OPPOSITE ABOVE: The flags are out in North End, Croydon, in the summer of 1945, as the war in Europe is over. Former Croydon Corporation E1 tram No 379, modernised by London Transport in the 1930s, is passing the entrance to Whitgift Middle School. Further back is a Feltham, also Purley-bound.

OPPOSITE BELOW: Single-deck routes have always been more common in the outer suburbs. A Leyland National on the 12A, a route that would eventually be replaced in this sector by the 412, heads along the boundary of suburbia and rural Surrey as it approaches its Riddlesdown terminus in July 1977.

BELOW: The one and only rear-engined Routemaster, FRM 1, was for a time allocated to Croydon garage and is seen here at Riddlesdown in 1971.

ABOVE: The 4.48pm Victoria to Brighton train was something of a flagship of the Oxted line, being favoured by returning businessmen; enthusiasts also relished the notion of travelling behind steam between London and Brighton. Here, D1 No 31739, hauling seven Maunsell corridors, has just emerged from Riddlesdown tunnel on 19 June 1961. To the best of the author's knowledge, this elderly, but highly efficient inside-cylinder 4-4-0 spent just two days on this duty before being replaced by a Schools and, later, a Bulleid Pacific.

OPPOSITE ABOVE: Schools Class No 30928 *Stowe* pauses at Sanderstead with the 4.48pm to Brighton, August 1961. The station was way down the valley towards Croydon and a long way from Sanderstead village. At that time, it marked the extent of the third rail, being the terminus of trains from Charing Cross and Elmers End.

OPPOSITE BELOW: Whyteleafe in 1939. In the distance, a Tilling ST, partly hidden by a GPO Morris van, is heading down the A22 Eastbourne to London road towards Purley, where it will join the A23 from Brighton. 'The Please Cross Here' signs beside the two ladies chatting pre-date Belisha-beacon crossings, while the most modern vehicle is an almost new Ford 10 saloon.

Croydon Transport

ABOVE: Abellio Alexander Dennis E40H 2583 of 2017 passing Whyteleafe South station on its way along the A22 to Caterham in December 2019.

OPPOSITE ABOVE: A 4-EPB unit from Charing Cross, East Croydon and Purley has just left Whyteleafe South and is heading towards its terminus deep in the North Downs at Caterham, c1974. The A22 is just visible on the far left. There were still plenty of semaphore signals to be found on the suburban network at this time.

OPPOSITE BELOW: Croydon-bound ST 1041 stands opposite Caterham station on its long journey from Forest Row, c1940. It retains full pre-war Country Area livery but has wartime white-tipped wings.

81

A 409 at the same location 61 years later, but on the opposite side of the road. Note the steepness of the road leading down from Caterham-on-the-Hill, which Arriva's MCW Metrobus M 559 has just negotiated. The absolute minimum of destination information would seem to be the order of the day.

Godstone garage on 27 October 1977, with a collection of Atlanteans, Fleetlines, a Routemaster and a Leyland National.

Oxted in 1975, with a six-car DEMU from London Bridge and East Croydon setting out for East Grinstead. A Reliant Robin shares the station yard with an interesting collection of vehicles in the sidings.

Tunbridge Wells West on 9 June 1961. H Class 0-4-4T No 31544 has charge of the two-coach 3pm to Oxted, with connections for Croydon. In the distance, behind the coal wagons, is the depot, and beside it is a 4MT 2-6-4T awaiting its next turn of duty.

A 12-coach DEMU from Victoria and East Croydon bound for East Grinstead, with unit No 1308 bringing up the rear, has just pulled out of Hurst Green in 1969 and is passing the junction with the Uckfield line. Normally, three or six carriages would suffice, but this is a race day at Lingfield.

An Uckfield to East Croydon and Victoria train, with diesel unit No 171730 leading, passes the junction with the East Grinstead line at Hurst Green on 8 June 2024.

RCL 2228 has broken down on Sanderstead Hill in 1975 and is about to be overtaken by RMC 1515, both from Chelsham garage.

RT 604, RCL 2240 and RT 1018 repose at Chelsham garage in 1978, all three in National Bus Company livery; as it happened, these were two of the only three London Country RTs to carry it into service, the other being RT 3461.

18
... and Hovis and butter for tea
Ty-Phoo TEA
CROYDON
PURLEY
1910

ICES TO LET
RST FLOOR
KINS & SONS
DAVIS
W.H.CU

Croydon Transport

OPPOSITE ABOVE: A crew change beside Purley depot in 1950. An LCC-built E3, dating from 1930, has almost completed its journey from the Embankment to Purley.

OPPOSITE BELOW: A Feltham passing the Davis Cinema, once the largest in the UK, in 1945. To the left of the tram, beyond the Ford 8hp saloon, is the entrance to Surrey Street market.

BELOW: Whatever has gone amiss with Croydon of late, its wonderfully colourful Surrey Street market remains a crowd-drawing attraction, and is seen here from a passing tram descending Crown Hill in 2023.

LEFT: How it all began; the statue of the Tudor Archbishop Whitgift, albeit somewhat weary-looking by now, sits outside Croydon Town Hall.

OPPOSITE ABOVE: A tram commemorating the 30th anniversary of the opening of the Whitgift Centre in 1970 and a matching blue Metrobus Volvo Olympian, West Croydon, 2001.

OPPOSITE BELOW: A Trinity School of John Whitgift pupil – note the archbishop's -mitre badge – on a visit to the Museum of British Transport, Clapham, in 1969, inspects preserved London Transport NS 1995.

Croydon Transport

ABOVE: Whitgift Middle School, which stood on the site of the Whitgift Centre until 1965.

OPPOSITE ABOVE: North and southbound 403s, RTs 2509 and 2510, meet at West Croydon on 21 May 1956. The 403 was one of the longest routes operated by London Transport, the journey from Wallington, deep in outer suburbia, to Tonbridge taking two hours and five minutes. The final ten or so miles were shared with services from Maidstone & District. Delivered in February 1950, the batch comprising RTs 2499–2521 was a familiar sight when new on the streets of Croydon; six were allocated to Dunton Green, 15 to Chelsham and two to Crawley. They gradually moved away over the years, some being repainted red. The last of all was RT 2504, which in London Country days was still working into Croydon on the 408 from Leatherhead garage.

OPPOSITE BELOW: A Victoria to Coulsdon North stopping train consisting of two 4-SUBs approaching its destination in 1968. Coulsdon had no less than three stations, the other two being Smitham on the Tattenham Corner branch and Coulsdon South on the line to Redhill. There were extensive sidings at Coulsdon North but these gradually fell out of use; services to the station also declined and finally ceased in 1983. The A23 Brighton Road now occupies the site.

CROYDON SANDERSTEAD
WARLINGHAM
WESTERHAM BRASTED
RIVERHEAD SEVENOAKS
HILDENBOROUGH
403
WALLINGTON STN
FRIARY ALES
FRIARY ALES
403
KXW 139
403
WARLINGHAM
WESTERHAM
SEVENOAKS
TONBRIDGE STN
HOLIDAY
DALTONS WEEKLY
Beer

4601
94

ABOVE: An N Class 2-6-0 heads south through Coulsdon North with a Redhill-bound freight in November 1954. The Ns were a mixed-traffic design originating on the SE&CR in 1917 and were added to by the Southern Railway, production continuing until 1934. A most useful class of engine, the last was withdrawn in 1964 and one has been preserved.

LEFT: RT 4280 at Haling Park Road, South Croydon, on a short working of the 109 to Westminster in 1973. The 109 replaced the 16/18 tram routes in 1951, carrying on the task of connecting Purley with Victoria Embankment (subsequently known as just Embankment in general use, for fear of confusion with the terminus beside Victoria railway station). It needed 62 buses, more or less equally divided between Brixton and Thornton Heath garages. Short workings were common, though the section between South Croydon and Purley was covered by several other routes and eventually disappeared altogether.

RIGHT: A westbound tram crosses the damp Park Lane underpass into George Street in October 2003. The church in the distance to the south, is St Peter's, which was constructed in the early 1850s by Sir George Gilbert Scott. The author once shared Christmas temporary employment duties with a trainee vicar who, in a previous existence, had been part of the planning team responsible for the underpass, of which he was rather proud.

BELOW: Full occupation of the three tram tracks at East Croydon station on 12 November 2003. One tram, No 2525, wears its original red and white livery, while the other two have all-over adverts, a feature of the new Croydon system since its inauguration. Towering over all is the distinctive tower block, No 1 Croydon, which was soon dubbed the 'Threepenny Bit' for its resemblance to that august coin. 269ft high with 24 storeys, designed by Richard Seifert and Partners and completed in 1970, it has become a symbol of the modern high-rise Croydon of the 1970s, through not necessarily a simultaneous object of admiration.

ABOVE: A Southdown Brighton-to-London Leyland Tiger coach passes London Transport Country Area RT 4787 at Coulsdon. Southdown invested in a large fleet of luxurious, mostly Harrington-, Park Royal- and ECW-bodied Leyland Tiger PS1 coaches in the immediate post-war years as travel to the Sussex coast boomed. The Park Royal or Weymann-bodied 56-seat RT was equally outstanding in its own field, comfort-wise, especially once it had been fitted with heaters upstairs and down.

OPPOSITE ABOVE: Passengers at Purley on a London Bridge-bound Saturday morning train in June 2024. Saturdays are now the busiest day on the Southern suburban network. Could they be going to a Taylor Swift concert?

OPPOSITE BELOW: At the very end of the steam era, Bulleid Light Pacifics appeared on passenger workings on the Oxted line. Bulleid Pacifics are rather like Marmite; some thought they were wonderful, whereas others felt that there were far too many of these complicated, failure-prone austerity-era machines that replaced small, elderly locomotives that could do the job more efficiently. Certainly they were not needed on the Oxted line. Nevertheless, No 34050 *Royal Observer Corps* makes an impressive spectacle as it approaches East Croydon in February 1961.

34050

Other books you might like:

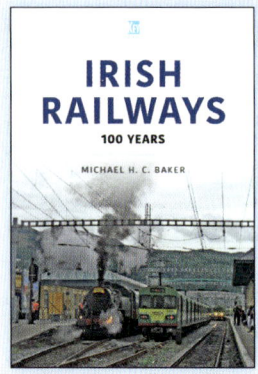

IRISH RAILWAYS
100 YEARS
MICHAEL H. C. BAKER
World Railways Series, Vol. 7

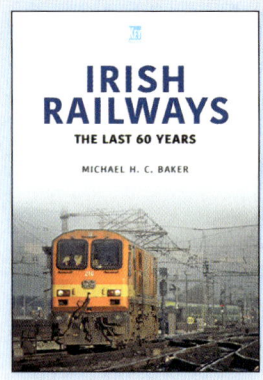

IRISH RAILWAYS
THE LAST 60 YEARS
MICHAEL H. C. BAKER
World Railways Series, Vol. 4

LONDON BUSES
REVIEW OF 2023
MATTHEW WHARMBY
Transport Systems Series, Vol. 12

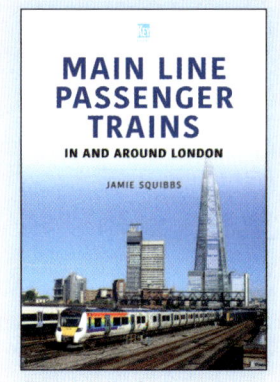

LONDON BUSES
REVIEW OF 2022
MATTHEW WHARMBY
Transport Systems Series, Vol. 8

LONDON BUSES
REVIEW OF 1998
MATTHEW WHARMBY
Transport Systems Series, Vol. 10

MAIN LINE PASSENGER TRAINS
IN AND AROUND LONDON
JAMIE SQUIBBS
Britain's Railways Series, Vol. 42

For our full range of titles please visit:
shop.keypublishing.com/books

VIP Book Club

Sign up today and receive
TWO FREE E-BOOKS

Be the first to find out about our forthcoming book releases and receive exclusive offers.

Register now at **keypublishing.com/vip-book-club**

Our VIP Book Club is a 100% spam-free zone, and we will never share your email with anyone else.
You can read our full privacy policy at: privacy.keypublishing.com